Healing Conversations

Healing Conversations

TALKING Yourself Out of Conflict and Loneliness

David Roberts

NASHVILLE

NEW YORK • LONDON • MELBOURNE • VANCOUVER

Healing Conversations

Talking Yourself Out of Conflict and Loneliness

Published in New York, New York, by Morgan James Publishing. Morgan James is a trademark of Morgan James, LLC. www.MorganJamesPublishing.com

ISBN 9781642797541 paperback
ISBN 9781642797558 eBook
Library of Congress Control Number: 2019911863

Cover Design by:
Rachel Lopez
www.r2cdesign.com

Interior Design by:
Christopher Kirk
www.GFSstudio.com

Morgan James is a proud partner of Habitat for Humanity Peninsula and Greater Williamsburg. Partners in building since 2006.

Get involved today! Visit
MorganJamesPublishing.com/giving-back

Table of Contents

Dedication

To all the people who have risked vulnerability to honestly share their lives and their stories, their authenticity has allowed me to learn, grow and better understand the gift and power of conversation.

Chapter 1

It's So Funny How
We Don't Talk Anymore

*In a world where we are able to instantly communicate
with anyone at any time and any place, we seem to
have less and less of substance to talk about.*

In 1979 Cliff Richard recorded a song entitled, "It's So Funny How We Don't Talk Anymore." The lyrics described a couple whose relationship was ending. It seemed that at one point life was sweet and they thought their relationship was complete, but now they were throwing it away. The chorus then got to the heart of the problem—finding humor in how they stopped talking and why they stopped talking. It's a fair question to think about, though it's not funny at all. Maybe it is worth asking, "How did we end up not talking anymore?" "Why did we end up not talking anymore?"

A few years ago, we were on a cruise ship in the port of Le Havre, France. My family and I were taking an excursion and met in a big theater on the ship with hundreds of others who would be taking once-in-a-lifetime trips to see some of the great wonders of the world. Imagine the potential sitting in that room. Some would tour the beaches of Normandy and surrounding countryside. Some would make their way into the interior of France and spend a day cooking and eating with a celebrated chef. Others were on their way to spend an entire day in Paris to visit The Louvre, see the Eiffel Tower, and eat at a French sidewalk cafe.

As we waited for our tour to be called an older couple a few rows in front of us began to argue. The conversation became heated. Voices rose. The intensity grew. It was clear they had reached an impasse, neither one being willing to bend. Just as it was becoming uncomfortable for those of us with front row seats to the spectacle, the couple's tour was called. They were among those who were scheduled to spend just one day, a few hours really, in Paris. She stood quickly and headed for the line. He sulkily remained in his seat. Everyone waited to see who would break. She resolutely stood in line, edging closer and closer to the exit door. A last call for the tour to Paris was made. Finally, the old man stood and spoke loud enough for his wife, now in the doorway to hear, "All right, I'll go, but I won't enjoy it!"

"It's so funny…"

Most of us have been there. Stuck in a relational battle where everyone loses. Whatever words were being exchanged by the couple, they were certainly not communicating. At some point there was no longer even any desire for resolution and mutual happiness. No, they were both stuck in what an author friend of mine calls, "The Right-Wrong Trap." They would rather be "right" than be "happy." Even the basic belief that *my* version of reality is right may speak to why it is we don't talk anymore. The longing to be right is deep and universal—we all want to be right, but too often being right leads us to dominate another and make them wrong. It moves from resolving the issue to winning and losing. We seem to move quickly into a willingness to punish and hurt. So, on a cruise ship, at a port in France, a small group of us watched a man and his wife in a tiny war and that made all of us a little miserable. It's so *awful* how we don't talk anymore.

Many of us having been through a few of those tiny wars have adopted a similar philosophy, "All right, I'll go, but I won't enjoy it!" I won't enjoy life. I won't enjoy the wonders of friends, family, good food, laughter, hope, joy and the privilege to be alive. I won't be happy. We're pretty sure it's not our fault. We're right. They're wrong. The need to win closes us down, shuts off communication and sabotages our own happiness. We all know if we are not intentional about being thankful and focusing on the good stuff, we easily find ourselves going, but not enjoying.

To fully understand what is happening inside of us and in the people around us we would need to talk about it, and we don't talk much anymore. It's not that we don't say words, but we seldom engage in meaningful conversations that help us understand the deeper inner worlds of the people with whom we are sharing life and also to better understand ourselves. So, why don't we talk?

There's Talk, and Then There's Conversation

Let's define our terms. Conversation is talk between two or more people in which thoughts, feelings and ideas are expressed. One of the roots of the word, according to the Online Etymology dictionary, says that; "conversation" from the mid-fourteenth century means "living together, having dealings with others and even the manner of conducting oneself in the world." The Latin literally means "to turn together." Is that what talking is achieving for you? Do the conversations in which you engage lead to a "turning together"?

We Talk for Three General Purposes

First, we talk to communicate information and navigate logistical issues. It's basic stuff. When are we leaving? What's for dinner? Do you need anything from the store? Although functional talking is basic to navigating our lives, it still requires caring attentiveness to be effective. We encounter a lot of conflict because we do not communicate the functional information clearly. Without listening and clearly articulating what we mean, functional talking can complicate the simplest of tasks. This is where many of our conversations devolve. These logistical conversations typically are not impassioned or emotional unless someone has messed up the information and we experience conflict. At those times the kind of "passion" that is revealed can be hostile and unsafe. If we can't safely talk about such low-level information, how will we ever approach the vulnerable space of our inner worlds?

Second, we talk to pursue an agenda. Think of this kind of conversation as "debate." In all honesty, how often do we open our mouths without an agenda, a goal, and a desired outcome in mind? We have decided. We place our needs at the center of most of our conversations. Why talk at all if not in pursuit of convincing others of our point of view, or to get something, or to create an effect? It's astonishing how much of our conversations live in this space. Often, even our logistical issues can become labored by agenda-driven words and expectations. In other settings we might call that passive-aggressive behavior. We rarely speak without some idea in mind about how we expect people to respond. Underlying this kind of communication is a deep-seated belief that *I get it, I'm right. The world would be a better place, my family would be happier; my friends smarter, if they would just listen to me and agree!*

The **third** distinct kind of conversation is relational talking, characterized by genuine hospitality. There is empty space within which conversation can thrive in order to build connections between people and families. These are conversations based on wanting to understand another person's life, emotions and journey. Empty space implies a place to talk without any agenda, judgment, or even preconceived ideas concerning the outcome. It's just free space, empty space to roam around and graze on ideas and thoughts, nuances and feelings.

Great relational talking ascends to art. It is much more risky and vulnerable than functional or agenda-focused talking. It pushes deeper into what makes each of us who we are. It dares to explore our struggles, our goals, purposes, and answering life's persistent questions. In this space, people want to define their terms and make sure the other person understands what they mean by their words. In this space, people long to be understood and strive to completely understand others. Words in this setting cause us to "turn together."

Why don't we converse like that? It's such a *waste* that we don't talk anymore.

What better way to "turn together" than in providing space for people to feel comfortable enough to be, to express themselves, to relax and open up. That requires true hospitality. A huge barrier to conversation is that so many of us have forgotten the nature of true hospitality and how to practice it.

How Are You at Hospitality?

Henri J.M. Nouwen has defined hospitality as:

> "...primarily the creation of free space where the stranger can enter and become a friend instead of an enemy. Hospitality is not to change people, but to offer them space where change can take place. It is not to bring men and women over to our side, but to offer freedom not disturbed by dividing lines."[1]

Every human being longs to be wholly himself; to be happy, to be known, not hidden, to love and to be loved, appreciated, understood, supported, celebrated and connected. In all the years I have served as a pastor I have never had anyone come into my office seeking loneliness. Some have come wishing they could be left alone, but no one wants to be lonely.

The key to being known and understood and ultimately to being loved as wholly oneself, is learning to communicate at the deepest and most intimate levels. If you stop and think it over, the primary way we can learn, grow, connect, understand

---

1   *Reaching Out,* by Henri J.M. Nouwen, pg.106, Doubleday 1975, N.Y., N.Y.

and become relationally involved is with our words. All of our understanding is built through communication, but the communication that builds understanding is sabotaged when we try to push personal agendas. Any hope of a relational conversation stops immediately. Intimacy is banished. Isolation is increased and disappointment grips our hearts once again. Even worse, we are experts at settling into patterns. The content of many conversations is predictable based on highly recognizable patterns.

Most of us feel the pinch of a coming interaction after the first few words. We begin a conversation, familiar patterns appear and we feel ourselves slipping into what feels like a pre-rehearsed script. Our conversation is no longer alive and spontaneous. We are almost on auto pilot as the all too familiar words replay once again. At this point, we are pulling up the defenses that have guided us through this conversation before. When these patterns emerge, the hope for a satisfying conversation seems remote or even hopeless. If we stopped in the middle of this mechanical conversation we would likely find our brains are focused on our defenses and our anxiety is high. These patterns undermine any hope of genuine hospitality, let alone a satisfying exchange.

Is it possible that we don't experience hospitality even in our homes? We don't converse as much anymore because we have neglected the finer points of hospitality. We may often find ourselves in a debate where someone is trying to convince us of something. We may even be privileged to enjoy a moment of discussion, but research tells us that usually discussions are dominated by those who talk the most. True dialogue, where we enjoy the warmth and comfort of genuine conversation is rare and precious.

Watch the evening news and the "talking" is not empty space or an exploration of ideas, but there you see, at worst, folks hurling words at one another, making weapons of words, and at best, talking heads pushing an agenda with the simple goal of being entertaining enough to build market share.

If you have the heart and stomach, scroll through some social media and observe the exchanges between so-called friends. Watch for argument-driven headings like: "This one gets it exactly right" or "This argument destroys the opposition." These days even some family gatherings have become settings for open debate about everything political, social, cultural and generational. Some family spaces have become so tension-filled that silence or superficial talk is the default setting. In any case, debate has become the default for most communication and it often pushes aside any real two-way conversations. There's rarely genuine empty space for exploration and expression. Debating too often lands people in the right-wrong trap. People assert with great passion that my idea, philosophy, point of view is right, and yours is wrong.

There was a time when the church seemed to understand that they were called to be the ultimate place of hospitality where everyone who was weak or heavy burdened could find a place to rest and be restored. Churches were places where people could celebrate their spiritual paths with honesty, inclusion and love. Churches were great role models of caring hospitality and safe places for people to unburden themselves or at least, converse deeply. And, some still provide this beautifully.

These last few decades, however, have seen more and more churches descend into places of debate over the most difficult political, social, cultural and generational issues. More and more churches are identified by which sides they choose, or what nuance they endorse. Churches and denominations are splitting apart as Bible verses are honed into weapons for the sake of proving a treasured theological point. This seems to be the priority rather than to provide a safe place for not only the weak and heavy burdened, but also for those searching and longing for self-knowledge, for understanding and for communing with others in a deeper way.

We Don't Want to Take the Time

Do you remember those squeaky swings and rocking chairs on porches, where guests or family members sat and talked, perhaps with a glass of sweet tea or lemonade? Somehow, there was all the time in the world and a comfortable space to catch up, tell stories, and just breathe together. This was a part of hospitality, to take the time to "be" with people.

Again, in a world where we are able to instantly communicate with anyone at any time in any place around the world, we seem to have less and less of substance to talk about. The more technologically capable we are in communicating, the less it seems we seek understanding and real conversation. On a global scale, or in our homes with our children and spouses, we seem to be losing our ability to deeply converse with each other. Are we losing touch with one another and with ourselves?

It doesn't matter if we're trying to improve a relationship with a co-worker, or discussing very personal issues with our spouse, or attempting to talk to a cross-armed teenager or working through a misunderstanding with a friend. In order to communicate, we must learn to talk in ways that heal our past wounds and open the door to deeper connection. In chapters eight through fourteen, we will suggest ways to bring this about. But first, I'd like to point out the struggles most people deal with—that they might bring to the table to begin a healing conversation. The first struggle we have all experienced is the restless feeling of being *unsettled.*

Chapter 2

Unsettled

How would you finish this sentence?
I had hoped by now my life would
be_____!

I love good stories. In the process of writing this book a friend and fellow writer shared this story with me. She had met a man who had an unsettled inner world. He was searching. In a most unexpected way, he encountered hope. As we talked more and more about the power of conversations to turn us together, the story took on more and more significance. I invited her to write it down and I invite you to reflect on it.

"I know a man who walked the whole night around Paris looking at his life: where he'd been, what he'd done, what he really wanted to accomplish. The rain was relentless and so were his gloomy thoughts about himself. Once in a while he'd step under the eaves of some building to shake out his umbrella and tighten the fine Scottish scarf around his neck. Twenty-eight years of age and educated, he still felt deeply unsettled. He had reflected for hours upon this realization; that his job was to find his passion and manifest some product or service into which he could pour that passion. He demanded answers from God; How? Where? What? As he walked and ruminated ideas, passions and purposes, things gradually began to come together. His mind was no longer filled with puzzle pieces that didn't seem to connect into a picture. Some pieces belonged to other people and were discarded, but the frame of the picture held, the image became clear.

At dawn, he dipped into a bakery, and somewhere between the first bite of a warm croissant and a satisfying sip of dark-roasted coffee, he also realized that he might always feel unsettled to some extent and that he wished he had someone in his life that he could talk to—really share the deep stuff. He did feel he was talking with God along the way of his walk, but there was a need for human connection that he missed. He'd just broken up with his girlfriend, and his parents didn't really understand his wanderlust or his life choices so far.

He looked at an older gentleman sitting at the tiny table next to him who had just set down his newspaper and who, at that instant, looked up at him and gave him a nod and a small smile. Could he dare to open a conversation with this gentleman? A little rush of excitement compelled him. And so, one glorious morning was spent sharing epiphanies with a stranger in a small café in Paris—the highlight of his journey."

I like the romance of that story. The lonely rainy streets of Paris, the quiet, lonely walk of a person who is searching, feeling lost; feeling the need to converse with God, to seek, to knock, but the unsettled human heart also needs someone with skin on and so did our young man. Sometimes strangers offer a safer place to process our thoughts, to hear our stories without prejudice and to offer us some deeply needed acceptance. Sometimes we receive guidance from strangers more willingly than from the people with whom we are currently sharing the journey.

At any age or time, we may find we need to be alone and take that long walk to reflect on our lives. Those times are usually motivated by a sense of feeling unfulfilled or unsettled in some way.

I am unsettled. Do you feel that way? I had hoped by now, having passed through so many milestones in my life, that life would be more tranquil. Just saying that sentence aloud feels unsettling. What an open-ended line of thinking. How would you finish the sentence? I had hoped by now my life would be_____!

I thought when I grew up that I would find myself more in control. In the musical, "Matilda," the lead girl sings about what she will be able to do when she grows up: reach the branches that would enable her to climb the tallest trees, be smart enough to answer the tough questions, be strong enough to carry all the heavy things and be brave enough to fight scary things.

I thought by now that I would have answers to many more questions, be strong enough to carry the burdens, and be brave enough to fight, but it seems those were unrealistic expectations. The questions got harder, the baggage heavier and the scary things even more frightening.

My inner world lacks the long sought-after sense of well-being. The problem must be deep in my inner workings because I can't seem to get a handle on what is making that odd thump in my soul. It's elusive. I've checked all the obvious things that often cause a sense of uneasiness; relationship tensions, health worries, overwhelming work and so on, but the sound is coming from someplace deeper.

I remember a time, years ago in graduate school, when I had a similar inner thump. Something within my mind constantly sent messages to my brain that I was never in the right place at the right time! I needed to study, that's what graduate school was all about; the season of preparation. I was in training for life and the future, but when I studied, the thump in my soul indicated I should be spending time with my young family. After all, my daughter was only two. These were priceless days and too soon they would pass. "Books will always be around." A voice said, "You can learn on the job, but your family is your first priority." Thump, thump, thump in my soul.

If I settled into quality family time, I could actually hear the bills demanding to be paid. *Hey, Buddy-boy, I'm over here, in this pile. Don't you dare pass me by; you're a responsible family man now!* What was I thinking? I didn't have time to study or sit around with the family; I needed to be working. "Defer school," I told myself. "Family time won't make much sense when we're homeless and hungry. You need a second job, maybe a third!"

I felt I was on a roller coaster ratcheting up and up. Reaching the top, the bottom dropped out and my inner voice screamed all the way down. At the bottom the cycle began again, "You should study more—that's the only reason you are even in this situation, to get an education—that's what graduate school is all about—this is the time of your life to prepare!" The soundtrack in my subconscious played like a Hitchcock thriller. I knew something bad was about to happen because I was being pulled and pushed into confusion by ominous voices and sounds of impending doom. Thump, thump, thump—like a metronome behind menacing music, increasing in volume. I was out of place emotionally, mentally and spiritually. I was big-time unsettled.

Oh, sure, looking back, I realize that despite the unsettledness, those days were good days—some of the best days of my life thus far. There was a simple and understandable cause to the unsettled feelings. There was a beginning, middle and an end to graduate school. Once graduation came, life would begin. I figured now that the hard work was done, life would just unfold in a matrix of work, marriage, children, domestic chores, dreams, vacations, politics, economics, life philosophies, spiritual fulfillment and we would all be happy, right? When I grow up!

Well, it turns out, life had already begun. The thumping noises and soundtrack did quiet down a bit. Life gave me many wonderful opportunities to grow. But, even as my voice matured, became stronger, more resonant and confident, even as I sometimes spoke with the authority of education and hard-won experience, despite my moments of clarity and insight, deep down in my machinery, the old, familiar thump in my soul sometimes still knocked around. On my worst days, there's a fear that I'm missing "it". That something precious is right in front of me, but I'm either too busy or too tired to see it. I just feel unsettled.

Does any of this sound familiar? I've always wondered if others felt a little thump in their souls too. Maybe it's just part of being human. Does it connect to a need for a person, a group, an identity, a profession, a place in life? Maybe some of us have something inside that makes us feel different, out-of-step, unsettled. I suppose that the feeling is sometimes a sense of not fitting in.

How many of us have an inner soundtrack that plays heightened music that serves as a warning that some sort of danger is just around the next corner? How many live with an anxious sense that we are not where we should be, the world is out of control and something is bound to jump out of the dark and get us? Are there those of us who sense we are on the wrong road, at the wrong time and too late we will finally see what's dead ahead? Will we wish we had turned right or left or made a U-turn a long time ago? If only we had chosen differently.

I believe that most people want the same things. I believe, across the board, across the world, across cultures, and religions, people largely want fundamentally good things. Many times, however, we just don't agree on how to get them. And in that chaos of not agreeing on how to get them, we've become polarized; we've become adversarial instead of cooperative.

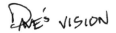

The Source of the Thump

After lots of thinking, searching and growing, I discovered the source of my thump. It is rooted in my unsettled inner world. The complexity of trying to find the right balance in life, and the truth, and the way forward required me to open up. I needed to talk about it. I needed safe places to process it all out, get input and find guidance. The source of the thump is all the built up confusion deep inside of me. I could unlock the confusion and quiet the thump by honestly sharing it in trusted relationships. However, sharing it can feel threatening because doing so often invites conflict or risks embarrassment. This insight, that sharing is important and necessary, but is also risky, adds to my unsettled feelings. I want to live in relationships where I am not afraid to be wholly myself. I want to be able to have conversations with those closest in my life without fear of rejection and without criticism or cynicism from them. I want connection; not eye rolls, frustration, generation gaps, and misunderstanding. The thump is the desire to be safe and at rest at the deepest relational parts of my soul. I think we all want to talk to our spouse without fear of conflict. I think we want to express ourselves to our children without inciting anger or disconnection, but the source of the thump is much deeper than that.

I long for things to be different *in our world*. Not only do I want to genuinely be myself and express my beliefs around my closest circle, but also around those who don't think just like I think and believe exactly what I believe. I find that as the world fractures and becomes fiercely divided, I have a deep longing for all of us to stay connected, a longing for things to come together in very personal and relational ways even as the world seems to be falling apart. I have to believe there is a purpose for such deep longing.

Chapter 3

Longing

*I find more and more people are longing to
connect, ready to get to know others and take
the risk to express themselves.*

I can't stop thinking about the man on the cruise ship I
talked about earlier. I long for him to soften and climb
out of the right/wrong trap; to take his wife's hand and
admit he was a bit of a jerk and to find a way to enjoy Paris
with his wife. I long for it the way I long for our world to be so
much less polarized and divisive, the way I long for us to find a
renewed sense of respect, connection and grace, to rediscover
conversations of dignity, curiosity and growth.

I have longings for our culture, our politics, our world,
our relationships, my world, and my life. Sometimes it's
hard to talk about longings because it may imply that we're

unhappy. We want so badly for things to be good. We want to be strong, to be okay.

I long for unity, collaboration, resolution and combined efforts leading to combined celebrations. But everywhere I look I see polarized views pulling us apart. I see extreme fanaticism creating endless wars abroad and here. The voices of much of our culture are mean, unfair, and ill-mannered and I'm sick of hearing them. What also sickens me is that people seem to love to take extreme positions and celebrate them and that's divisive. Extremes often create polarization that ends in disharmony, anger and even intense fighting.

The Divisiveness of Extremes

In my experience, very few people are excited about the more mundane processes of life. There are no shows on TV, for example, where we watch someone learning to ride a bike; working through the process of finding balance, gathering momentum, and gaining stability. A majority of people will watch all day as people who have mastered a bicycle or skateboard or motorcycle show off death-defying skills that stagger our imaginations. People love extreme sports.

And, we like celebrating results much more than process. That tendency shows up in a lot of places, but let's linger with sports for a minute. We are not very interested in the regular season—it has become simply a prelude to the playoffs. We tune in for the championships and the upsets. The big crowds are drawn to the final game where the clear winner is crowned. The neglect of process and the devotion to winners seem to sharply divide the competitors into the very broad categories of winners and losers. It isn't logical, but we rarely have warm thoughts for second place. These all or nothing celebrations often leave fans feeling that it is less painful to be eliminated early than to be eliminated at the end.

It has become easy to see other aspects of our world through these same simplistic, extremist eyes. We see issues, causes and, of course, teams and tribes in terms of winners and losers. I mean, take politics. It is so much simpler to neatly divide everything between winners and losers, right and wrong, enlightened and uninformed. The culture seems completely comfortable with this polarized thinking. We are for or against, pro or con, conservative or liberal, and on and on the labels go. What happened to enjoying the process? Watching people learn their craft, finding their way, or forming their ideals is no longer interesting to most. The idea that we would raise up a group of people who are valued precisely because they are deeply committed to healthy processes would be a major shift in our cultural leanings.

Extremism has found its way into our relationships and impacts our ability to communicate without stress or fear. People, with longings to know and be known and to be wholly themselves and happy, have before them the daunting task of navigating extremism. The winner-take-all culture is threatening to put an end to all meaningful conversations about politics, moral issues, relationships, entertainment, art, spirituality or anything remotely related to the meaningful things in life. Such conversations are only safe for the strongest and surest.

Too many people feel empty and alone. Why? So many of our conversations have devolved into trivial interactions, and these are not significant, relevant, engaging, life-building, energizing and seldom ever fun. It is too dangerous to talk when the only acceptable outcome is to name the winner and the loser. Few of us can even remember the last time we had a sincere, life-giving conversation that actually offered us an opportunity to learn and grow. What is left in us is a profound sense of longing. It is a longing to know and be known at the deepest, most true level, and that requires vulnerability. We long to turn together.

Longing to Trust Politics

Politically, it feels as if we are more interested in making inflammatory statements about an opposing party than any cohesive statement about our country. Parties have become the ends in themselves as opposed to the means by which we establish a better world! I know most of us immediately think, "It's not us, it's them!" Our politicians ask us to ignore their personal lives, but then ask us to buy into their politics. How can we trust them if we don't know the people behind the rhetoric? Or, if we do know them and they have reprehensible personal lives, how can we trust them in office?

It is easy to highlight acts of inconsistency and misjudgment of those with whom we disagree and ignore such behavior from those with whom we agree. But let's be honest, we trust few of the people who report on politics and even fewer of the politicians. And yet, we embrace our politics with a moral passion. A purely objective view (if such a thing were possible) would likely reveal that each side manipulates its constituencies with carefully selected issues that keep them impassioned and connected.

Longing to Be Told the Truth

This leads me to another piece of the source of my unsettledness; I long to be told the truth. Just for once, wouldn't it be nice to hear the unbiased truth of a situation, to trust the source completely? The uncertainty is so overwhelming that many go so far as to decide there is no such thing as absolute truth. It's a natural response. Truth, by its definition would be something that reliably works in all situations. Given our limited perspectives, who can say with any certainty and honesty that some truths are always true? That is unsettling.

I was taught that the search for truth was not an arranged drive forward through a narrow cattle chute to a predetermined outcome. The search for truth was an all-out quest of the soul in all directions. The very idea that seeking and hungering after righteousness, i.e. rightness and truth, should be an inviting exploration that naturally leads to some greater and shared truth feels naive. What passes for wisdom today seems to depend on which agenda you've adopted instead of the proverbial, "higher good."

Truth and Religion

Religion hasn't been much better. The church has to accept its share of the blame for agenda-driven behaviors. As a person who's grown up in church, been educated and spent my career within its inner workings, I have seen times and situations where the willingness to search for truth was conspicuous by its absence. Religion, in many of its forms, is regarded with suspicion and considered by many to be a highly prejudiced source of misinformation and outdated propaganda.

With that said, it is important to take note that religion has done miraculous good in the world with a stunning record of attending to people in trouble through huge numbers of hospitals, and organizations devoted to refugee aid, catastrophe relief, clean water and all other poverty/illness/hunger-fighting needs facing our world. Few of us realize the staggering number of these life-giving works which are run, funded and staffed by churches and religious organizations. If you've been associated with religion you've seen the good and the criticisms seem largely unfair. But if you've been wounded by religion or are indifferent, you might be more prone to see the harm in it. It would be accurate to say that both of those perspectives have some truth in them even though they are almost completely opposite. This illustrates the complexity of trying to get to the truth. Opposing views, drawing on personal experience, provide a level of truth, but still leave us wide open to conflict.

Truth and Education

Educational institutions still seem to maintain a reputation for a wide-open pursuit of truth, but more and more, that pursuit can only involve the currently acceptable social or scientific theory. Philosophical thought within the higher education system seems often to be adversarial toward any explanation of the world, other than the "proven scientific method." Often any thought of faith or the ancient pursuit of meta-physics as a source of guidance is thought to be naive and laughable. The wide-open pursuit of truth in education can only proceed if that truth is well within the current dogma and already contained in the prescribed curriculum! After so much confusion and so many agendas, many of us withdraw and turn inward. Few other places are safe and at least we know that we are sincerely looking for the truth.

Truth in Social Interactions

Perhaps socially we could interact together and find some common ground, except that we're too impatient to undertake that in a genuine way. In order to discover truth in community we would need people with diverse perspectives and a variety of views. We should also include the undecided. Of course, we don't like to share community with people who don't think like us or share our opinions and too often people who don't know exactly what they think are given no voice. Who has time to wait around and help someone sort their thoughts, find their words? It's risky to consider all sides of an argument and be undecided. Try posting your search for truth or explore what you think on Facebook, Instagram, and Snapchat. See what kind of encouraging support you get for your courageous search!

Mental and emotional confusion mounts as we are subjected to the push and pull of a culture that seems to be the most unforgiving and judgmental in history. Psychologically, it's a difficult culture in which to live if you truly care about the state of the world beyond your own agenda. Given this type of a world, it is no wonder people find it challenging to feel at home or safe or to fit in anywhere.

Where Do the Mermaids Stand?

There's a wonderful story about fitting in from Robert Fulghum's great book, *All I Really Need to Know I Learned in Kindergarten.* He wrote:

"Giants, Wizards, and Dwarfs was the game to play. Being left in charge of about eighty children, age seven to ten years old, while their parents were off doing parenty things, I mustered my troops in the church social hall and explained the game. It's a large-scale version of Rock, Paper and Scissors, and involves some intellectual decision making. But, the real purpose of the game is to make a lot of noise and run around chasing people until nobody knows which side you are on or who won. Organizing a roomful of wired-up grade-schoolers into two teams, explaining the rudiments of the game, achieving consensus on group identity—all this is no mean accomplishment, but we did it with a right good will and were ready to go.

When the excitement of the chase had reached a critical mass, I yelled out, 'You have to decide now which you are—a GIANT, a WIZARD, or a DWARF!' While the groups huddled in frenzied, whispered consultation, a tug came at my pants leg.

A small child stood there looking up, and asked in a small, concerned voice, 'Where do the mermaids stand?'

Where do the mermaids stand? A long pause. A very long pause. 'Where do the mermaids stand?' says I.

'Yes. You see, I am a mermaid.'

'There are no such things as mermaids.'

'Oh, yes, I am one!'

She did not relate to being a giant, a wizard, or a dwarf. She knew her category, *mermaid*, and was not about to leave the game and go over and stand against a wall where a loser would stand. She intended to participate wherever mermaids fit into the scheme of things. Without giving up dignity or identity, she took it for granted that there was a place for mermaids and that I would know just where.

Well, where DO the mermaids stand? All the "mermaids"—all those who are different, who do not fit the norm and who do not accept the available boxes and pigeonholes? Answer that question, and you can build a school, a nation, or a world on it. What was my answer at that moment? Every once in a while, I say the right thing, 'The mermaid stands right here by the King of the Sea!' (Yes, right here by the King's Fool, I thought to myself.) So, we stood there, hand in hand, reviewing the troops of wizards, and giants and dwarfs as they roiled by in wild disarray. It is not true, by the way, that mermaids do not exist. I know at least one personally. I have held her hand."[2]

Fulghum is so right, answer the question of where the mermaids stand and you could change the world. The longing to belong is intense.

---

2   *The Mermaid* from ALL I REALLY NEED TO KNOW I LEARNED IN KIN-DERGARTEN: FIFTEENTH ANNIVERSARY EDITION RECONSIDERED, REVISED, & EXPANDED WITH TWENTY-FIVE NEW ESSAYS by Robert Fulghum, copyright © 1986, 1988 by Robert L. Fulghum. Used by permission of Ballantine Books, an imprint of Random House, a division of Penguin Random House LLC. All rights reserved.

Longing to Be Known

As I listen to people open their hearts and tell their stories I have become convinced that we all share very similar longings. We want to belong and to fit in. We want to have a place where we can be wholly ourselves and happy. This desire draws us toward an ideal and mythical place called home. We want rest, peace, safety and the assurance that we belong and that we are wanted.

When Jesus extends the invitation, "Come to me all you who are weak and heavy burdened," that speaks to a deep place in us. Perhaps every human being on the planet can relate, because we are creatures of longing. This desire for connection and unconditional love is built into our DNA and spirits even before birth. We are formed in the womb with an intricate, miraculous relationship to our mothers. When we are born, a doctor or midwife helps us find air, and the cord is cut, temporarily disconnecting us from our mothers. But in a few moments we are returned to mother with an inborn urge to find sustenance necessary to our body's growth. We crave closeness, but that simple need to connect gets more complicated right away.

It has to be said that we humans, being human, can easily damage this wide open need to connect and be known. The frustration of parents who are overwhelmed by the baby that cries too much, or doesn't sleep, or is just curious and into everything can send a message that leaves the baby feeling lonely, wrong, or deserving of disconnection. *If I reach out and am rejected, I must be wrong in some way.* This adds a monkey wrench to the innocent desire to connect. Maybe this baby figures he has to smile, giggle and charm the big people even more than usual into loving him, making him feel safe. Or maybe he withdraws a little from his desire to connect, to belong, to know and to be known. As he grows, the disapproval, disappointment and disgust from parents, elders, and teachers accumulates and he or she, who only ever wanted safe connection, a place to discover himself, to express himself honestly, now has a much more complicated inner world. If well-meaning parents just trying to raise healthy, balanced children, out of their humanness, can hinder the child in his reaching out, imagine what happens when the complications of life beyond a healthy family get hold of us.

Yet, having been privileged to hear the deeper stories of dozens and dozens of people, even after all we go through most people still have a very deep longing *to love and be loved, to know and be known, and ultimately, to belong.* I find that many of these people recognize the risk in pursuing this kind of belonging. We don't want to risk exposure. Yet, how will we ever belong if we do not disclose our truest selves?

BAD LEADERS CAN MANIPULATE THIS LONGING

What's Right about Longing?

What if having a deep sense of longing is a gift and not really something to hide and be ashamed of? People with a thump in their souls are uncertain and they long for something better, stronger, deeper and more satisfying. The longing to know and be known is not something to be dreaded, but to be embraced, discussed and even celebrated. Longing can lead to reaching out for things we deeply need in order to survive.

Vulnerable, thoughtful and brave souls just might start a beautiful change that celebrates the process of becoming, growing, changing, listening and learning. I find more and more people are longing to talk—ready to connect, ready to get to know others and take the risk to express themselves. Something deep in our soul aches for the sacred place called home where we can lean in—show attentiveness and respect, creating the space to know and be known.

Sometimes our first step toward reaching out is to take a little step toward the safety of a group. We hope that our longing might be satisfied by finding a tribe in which to find acceptance and approval. Let's examine the pluses and minuses of this desire to submerge ourselves in a group.

Chapter 4

Longing to Find a Tribe

*In choosing a tribe, we are both able to connect and
yet keep ourselves safe from full disclosure.*

When I was ten years old, I attended an all-boys'
summer camp. We were divided into four teams
that moved around the camps' activities on
a certain schedule. One team played sports while another did
crafts, while a third went to classes and the fourth got to visit the
camp store for ice cream, soda and candy.

That camp took place in deep East Texas in the middle
of summer. It was hot and humid and everyone looked forward to the rotation that finally led their team into the camp
store. There was a problem in communication at this camp,
however. Nobody really explained all the finer points of the
rules of the camp. They explained that you had to go with

your team and participate, but they never mentioned that you couldn't participate with your team *and* jump in with another team, too.

On one of those hot summer afternoons we finished sports a little early. We were just sitting outside under the trees doing nothing. I was watching while another team was entering the camp store. I had my camp money in my pocket. My ten-year-old brain told me there wasn't anything wrong with running over, buying an ice-cold soda and rejoining my team. I was a paying customer. I wasn't neglecting my responsibilities.

So, I jumped up and ran to the store. I got in line. I was polite and waited my turn. I ordered up my chosen refreshment and offered up my payment.

That's about the time I heard a booming voice say, "Hey, you're not on this team! You can't be in here right now. You're not allowed to buy anything."

The humiliation was instant. The counselor should have known better. He could have found a thousand better ways to let me know the finer points of the law. Instead he called me out right in front of everyone. All eyes turned on me. Suddenly I was a cheater, a malcontent and a troublemaker. Wait! I was never a troublemaker. In that instant I dropped the goods on the counter and felt the deep need to escape.

I remember lowering my head and in self-defense, muttering under my breath as a last-ditch effort to save a little dignity. For some reason muttering seemed to preserve some secret identity that was stronger than the humiliation I was experiencing. I had almost reached the door when that same sensitive leader came after me. He said, "You get out of here

MISUNDERSTOOD INTENTION (9)

and rejoin your team. And listen, we don't use that kind of language around here!"

The humiliation was complete. Now I was not only characterized as a cheat and a malcontent, but swore like a sailor when cornered. The only thing was, I hadn't actually uttered a single word. I could have spoken up and offered an explanation for why I was there and what I was thinking, but my instinctive reaction to the threatening situation of not belonging was to hide and to mutter.

That's an isolated little story, but it still holds power years later. I can still feel my hot embarrassment and the condemning stares of my peers and the unfair assumptions of those in authority. As a ten-year-old boy, something in me wanted to hide, to escape the conflict. The whole scene came about because of lack of good, reliable information that led to my being misunderstood, falsely accused, and publicly humiliated. I turned inward, hid and ran. Feeling great shame, I also soaked in resentment. No good life lesson came out of it—just a searing memory of embarrassment. More than one night in the ensuing years I replayed that humiliating moment. In the replays I was strong, articulate, rational and direct. For so many of us that is when we are most articulate and rational and direct, in the replays, right? But in the heat of the moment, we still find it most natural to hide, mutter and turn inward.

We want the hurting party to know that there is a "somebody" inside our skins. And then, in an act of self-defense, we make the self-destructive decision. *You don't get to know me because you have hurt me.* I am shocked at how natural it is to hide in the face of unfair treatment.

Groups Meet Certain Needs

The most appealing and universal path, to meet both the need to reach out and the need to hide from exposure of our deepest selves, is to join a tribe. A tribe is any sort of group which shapes our identity. The group meets two very opposing needs in us; the need to belong and be accepted and the need to hide in plain sight. As in Fulgrum's story, we can become wizards, giants, dwarfs or mermaids. There are endless choices of tribes in our world. They begin in very broad categories such as Conservative, Liberal, Democrat, Republican, Libertarian, religious, or non religious, but can narrow into incredibly well-defined affinity groups. For example, within religion you can choose any number of world religions. Let's say we choose Christianity. Within that, you could broadly choose Protestant, Catholic, Eastern Orthodox, Anglican or Coptic. Each layer, denomination or theological talking point is vetted over centuries to allow us to discern what sets of beliefs we find in each tribe and we can specialize endlessly. And then there are sports. Sports take us into many sub-categories: Professional or College, SEC or PAC 10, MLB, even Little League.

Longing to Find a Tribe

As I've said, in choosing a tribe, we are able to connect and yet keep ourselves safe from full disclosure. Before acceptance into a tribe, we agonize sometimes on how to present ourselves.

We decide to put on a happy face despite the fact that we've experienced many rejections. We've also inflicted rejections on others, which further inhibits our freedom to just easily belong. So, we come with a heart burdened with issues. We carry fear of having our transgressions and weaknesses discovered. We work to repress our shadow sides, our unresolved feelings, the losses and hurts. We come to the tribe with a pretense that we are clean and carefree. We believe this makes us more acceptable.

Choosing a tribe is a perfect way to hide in plain sight. It satisfies our need to belong, kind of. It gives us a sense of identity, sort of. It allows us to know and be fully known, in theory. This attempt to belong by selecting a tribe is not just a practical decision, it is emotional. We have a very deep longing to put an end to our feelings of disconnection and loneliness. The tribe choosing satisfies a need to belong, but to the extent we are hiding who we are, it also allows us to maintain a very real sense of anonymity. While it feels safe, it is also lonely. Often, the well-defined attributes of a group can be confining and demanding. Choosing a tribe can sometimes be complicated.

Emo Phillips captures this reality very well.

"Once I saw this guy on a bridge about to jump.

I said, 'Don't do it!'

He said, 'Nobody loves me.'

I said, 'God loves you. Do you believe in God?'

He said, 'Yes.'

I said, 'Are you a Christian or a Jew?'

He said, 'A Christian.'

I said, 'Me, too! Protestant or Catholic?'

He said, 'Protestant.'

I said, 'Me, too! What franchise?'

He said, 'Baptist.'

I said, 'Me, too! Northern Baptist or Southern Baptist?'

He said, 'Northern Baptist.'

I said, 'Me, too! Northern Conservative Baptist or Northern Liberal Baptist?'

He said, 'Northern Conservative Baptist.'

I said, 'Me, too! Northern Conservative Baptist Great Lakes Region, or Northern Conservative Baptist Eastern Region?'

He said, 'Northern Conservative Baptist Great Lakes Region.'

I said, 'Me, too! Northern Conservative Baptist Great Lakes Region Council of 1879, or Northern Conservative Baptist Great Lakes Region Council of 1912?'

He said, 'Northern Conservative Baptist Great Lakes Region Council of 1912.'

I said, 'Die, heretic!' And I pushed him over!'"

Groups Offer Safety

Safety exists in numbers. We can connect with people who agree with us and enjoy things in common. We can feel valued and have a sense of safety belonging with people. However, because we join the group, people assume we agree completely with the values and actions of the group. They do not ask us for full disclosure of who we are or what we believe, which is good because so much of the time, we don't know or we know, but don't want anyone else to know.

Groups Can Simplify Life

One of the greatest benefits of being connected to a tribe is that in an ever-complicating world, they simplify life. It is so much easier to neatly divide everything between us and them, winners and losers, right and wrong, enlightened and uninformed. It takes so much less brain power to navigate my world if I eliminate the gray. If I can see issues, causes, and personal arguments only in terms of winners and losers, then I don't have to wrestle with the difficult questions. I don't have to say, "I don't know." There is comfort in agreement and affirmation, and finally I can settle the issue of what is right. Of course, as more and more people identify with increasingly diverse groups, we are forced, in the face of such diversity, to say fondly, "I have settled on what's right *for me!*" I don't have to listen to contradictions anymore. Tired and confused, I have been manipulated enough. Our original pursuit of truth ends in the land of agreement, affirmation and "true enough."

We give our chosen tribe our measured loyalty. In return, they give us companionship, common goals, interests and beliefs, and very often, a complete package of what to think. In a world that expects us to have answers, this is invaluable. As a culture, we seem to have found a way to meet both the need to reach out and the need to hide in plain sight, protecting from exposure of our deepest selves. In choosing a tribe we long to be accepted and acceptable. We desire to find a place to express ourselves, to be valued and to find connection. So, groups and tribes have value. But belonging to them has complications and dilemmas.

Three Dilemmas

This process of tribe-choosing presents us with certain dilemmas. I will highlight three of them.

First, people get emotionally invested in their tribe and sometimes this means abandoning reason. As the pastor of one Christian church for several decades, I live among the people of this community and I know the people of this particular church. I know enough about the individuals to know that we are a wide-ranging and diverse group of people. These people represent the range of politics, social philosophies, economic strategies, and even would have differing opinions about what passes for orthodoxy in the church. Yet, we all gladly identify as one tribe. If you pick on us as a group, we can impressively band together for the well-being of the group, but we are not all alike and the individuality of the people in the group is often ignored. That may be because we have an emotional investment that our group should be of one accord.

This is true of most religious or political groups. There is great diversity within, but attack the group and the emotional response is fierce. At an extreme, a person might secretly feel, "I don't agree with everything this group stands for, but if you, as an outsider criticize my group, I will tear you apart."

There is a pretense of "oneness." And, the group often fails to feed a person's need for expression of his or her individuality. To think that any one group can provide us with a complete sense of belonging or provide a place where we can be completely known, is false and down deep we know that. But we tend to cling harder to convince ourselves that we've found the right fit. It makes us rather defensive and emotional about our turf. If you identify as a Democrat you are opposed to all those that throw stones at your chosen tribe even if you really don't believe everything for which your tribe stands. The Republicans are the same, but in any case, we get emotional because we are finding some sense of belonging in these tribes. That applies to all tribes—from Rotary to Kiwanis, to sports teams, to social justice groups and on and on the list goes. People are emotionally invested in their tribe, even if they don't really embrace everything about that tribe. This leads to point number two.

Second, tribes tend to be "one size fits all." When we identity with a tribe we are marrying the whole family and its array of ideas. Some points of view are very much who we are and how we feel. Others are not us at all, but we chose a tribe and take the bad with the good. Tribe-choosing can become a trap. Our longing to belong pushes us to choose and our need to stay anonymous encourages this hiding in plain sight, but it doesn't allow us much freedom to really talk together about what is inside of us. Instead we talk the expected talk and walk the expected walk. So, we choose the tribe for better or worse, and then hide in plain sight. We tend to let the group represent our perspectives. We don't agree with it all, but we need to belong and so we compromise.

Third, we admire the simplicity of group-speak. Most of us desire to be confident about our personal positions on the issues. We struggle individually to be completely resolute about how the world works, so the group becomes our confident voice. The complex issues that are hitting our world and our inability to get some kind of unbiased guidance on our positions leave us feeling overwhelmed. We don't really trust anyone's facts, but given the choice, we'll believe our tribe first. We want to be sure and confident and correct. We use the group as a substitute for our own self-confidence because we believe that being confused or uncertain is undesirable. Many times I've wished I was as well-adjusted, confident and certain of my position as most of the other tribe-choosers seem to be. There's a prejudice that goes with being unsettled and the acute longing that comes with that. That prejudice suggests that my longing is a sign of weakness.

Tribe choosing moves us away from isolation and into a space where we have some sense of belonging. We tend to let the group speak for us because it feels more confident and simple. Sadly, as our insides look at other people's outsides we conclude that other people's longings to belong are being met and satisfied by the tribe. When you slow down, and really listen to the stories of others, you start to hear a very familiar sound. Many, many people that you know; whether conservative or liberal, progressive, religious or non-religious, are not at all certain about life. They are ill at ease and live with a troubling thump in their souls. I have come to believe that this longing is what we all truly share in common.

As I said earlier in the book, we all long to know and be known. We all want to belong and want to fit in. We want to have a place where we can be wholly ourselves and happy. The desire draws us toward an ideal and mythical place called home. We want rest, peace, safety and the assurance that we belong.

Tribal Conflict

The tender, deep longing to connect and be ourselves, to be loved and appreciated hasn't gone away. Our chosen tribe might help. If it doesn't, we find a new tribe, but we are highly sensitive to our tribe being in conflict with an opposing tribe. Opposing points of view feel very threatening. Though we don't embrace all of our tribe's beliefs, we find ourselves defending them. Opposing perspectives are generally thrown around in extremes with all the subtlety of hand grenades. The arguments drive us deeper into beliefs that are not really ours, but they are better than the craziness that is assaulting us.

Finding ourselves in the middle of these complicated and heated debates reminds us of our need to belong and have some kind of protection. The insecurity of being let out in the open without ready answers is terrifying. We may not agree with the extreme positions presented to us, but it feels far more dangerous to be undecided and all alone, not belonging to any tribe at all. It seems the conflict has moved beyond a person-to-person kind of conflict. Today it seems the tribes fight and we follow.

In summary, tribe choosing moves us away from isolation and into a space where we have some sense of belonging, but it also isolates us from other points of view. It can easily cause us to be unwilling to listen, change and grow. When we reconsider the thump in our souls, we acknowledge that it comes, in part, from the longing for the world to be drawn together instead of falling apart into catastrophe. Choosing a tribe and living in its "one size fits all" reality rarely satisfies our deeper longing. And the tender, deep longing to connect and be ourselves, to be loved and appreciated, to love and appreciate others hasn't gone away. Most importantly, tribal life seems to push us further and further from turning together.

There is another logical way to fight our fears, insecurities and the uncertainties we feel in life. This possibility is more personal, but still allows us to hide in plain sight. We can simply choose a persona, a package of personality traits that feels inviting, safe and comfortable. We might not be entirely authentic, but it's much safer than being one's self.

Chapter 5

Hiding in Our Chosen "Type"

Do you hide behind a type, a persona, a mask, a synthetic personality?

Who are you really? How did you get to be who you are? Did you choose it? Did you evolve into the person you have become? Does the role seem chosen for you? Do you like who you have become? There is a need in every one of us to know and be known; to love and be loved. We want to be able to achieve full disclosure; to reveal our innermost selves and to be loved for who we really are, but there is also a need to protect ourselves from the dangerous people who can so easily damage us. Signing up with a tribe is a convenient way to belong and be protected at the same time. It's a good way to hide in plain sight. There is another easily accessible way to hide in plain sight; just chose a "type" of person to be, then grab a persona or mask and hide behind it or choose an identity that may fit for a while but then becomes confining.

It is fairly easy to place people into "types." There may be six and half billion people on the planet, but there are not all that many types of people. The Meyers-Briggs Type Indicator suggests there are sixteen personality possibilities. Of course, each of these can have their own variations, but that's a finite number given the vast number of people in the world. The personality inventories and the whole process of the social sciences, work because there is a finite and predictable sampling of people-types in the world. Most of us can say with a bit of judgement or condescension, "I know the type!"

I grew up in church and have been in churches my whole life, stretching now into five decades. All churches have types. In addition, there are roles that need to be played in churches and every church has role players. At every church there is the greeter whom everyone knows and is very often the person they first meet. There is the board member who always needs more information and causes meetings to run long! There are the people who drop in and are always repairing something. There are musicians and wanna-be musicians.

From church to church they go by different names and their personalities may be slightly different, but there is more alike about them than is different. It feels that I can now walk into almost any congregation and in pretty short order name the cast of characters and the roles they play in that particular setting. There's nothing negative about this, it just speaks to the reality that for most of us we fit into a type.

I don't think this is unique to churches. The same phenomenon occurs in offices, factories, sports teams and every other organization where human beings participate. That was true when I was in school. We had broad categories of type. Growing up in Texas in the '70s, we had popular kids, athletes, cowboys, band kids, brainiacs, losers, the class clowns and the rest of us who didn't seem to have a group. The social structure was highly defined by type. It saved time and energy in socializing if people could be broken down into types. We found identity and order in this process of typing people. I'm not suggesting this is in any way scientific or even accurate, i.e., that all people fit neatly into those roles, but roles do exist and are fairly easy to identify.

Caricatures of Type

This typing is so common and universally known that comedy is often built around the parody of types. *Saturday Night Live* built a show that has stretched over five decades creating genuine comedy and satire in the caricature of types. The list of skits from: Daily Affirmations with Stuart Smalley, Mom Jeans, Church Chat, Debbie Downer, The Nerds, the I.T. guy, all reminded us of people we knew who lived in those types.

Movies use this same caricature of type to make us laugh. Will Ferrell is a master with titles like, *Anchorman*, *The Legend of Ricky Bobbie*, and *Blades of Glory*. While these characters are over the top, we find them funny precisely because we identify with the types they represent. We seem to universally say, "I know the type!"

Roles Are Powerful Tools

Studies tell us that one of the top reasons given for divorce in this country is role-confusion. Decades ago society defined the role of a husband and a wife in very specific and narrow ways. There are many reasons to be thankful that those old strict role definitions have passed away, but the void left behind is a problem too. If couples admit that role confusion is a factor in the decision to end a marriage, it is a confession that they and also we no longer inherently know how to play the part of the husband or wife. Maybe we never did, but we used "types" to bridge the gap until we figured it out for ourselves. Types play a big part in helping us figure out who we are.

Safety in a Chosen Identity

What happens when our searching, unsettled, longing, inner worlds are exposed to the exciting possibilities of choosing a type? We feel hope. We feel a sense of direction and that's good. The problem comes when we substitute being a type for getting to know who we truly are and being that person in all family, work and social settings. This is most obvious when a person who feels uncertain, weak or like a failure, looks around for a winning identity to adopt. Here, we might see a broken, scared kid choose the role of a bully, because being dominant is more favorable than being vulnerable. Or the woman who, feeling unloved, unseen or lost becomes obsessed with some aspect of her physical appearance.

Molly had been in my office and generously allowed me to share her story of her adopting a persona. This persona was a mask or façade that satisfied the demands of her group, but did not represent her inner personality.

"I was always a shy girl, but by sixth grade I had a fierce longing to fit in and be liked—a normal scenario, of course. But for me I felt hollow and desperate. So, I watched the popular girls: their intentions, objectives and actions and I went on quite a campaign to create out of myself that winning identity. My observation and innate acting ability paid off and I succeeded. But it was a persona, a mask and I was empty behind it. Oh, I was a great imitator; I became popular, the cheerleader, elected to this and that, sought after by the boys, but it was mostly an act. That "winner" was in-authentic and though I did call on my own abilities to pull it off, I felt the phony, the cheat, the imposter.

And then I found a purpose and engaged my talent and skills in dance and acting. I was the quiet, introvert again and it was okay. I became acutely focused, at least for those classes, rehearsals and shows. I had nothing to prove because I was being myself. Still, outside of theater and dance, I fell back into that winning, synthetic identity whenever I felt insecure—for example, as an incoming fresh-man in college. Moving thousands of miles away to a culture that wasn't me, became a kind of hell, where I became lost in a role and my inner life got more and more secret and raw, sad with longing for something I felt was out of reach. Even the iden-tity of actor or dancer no longer gave me much joy because the competition was fierce and my insecurities flared and burned. In that inner darkness, all my longings, my real, deep longings got acted out in the most secretive of eating disorders—bulimia. I became addicted to this solution.

Despite the anxiety that plagued me, I yearned for help, so I mustered the courage and sought it. It took some trial and error to find the counselor that saw me behind the façade and believed I could shine through and succeed as myself. Years of conversations with that skilled, compassionate counselor helped me to unearth who I was and eventually understand and love the true self beneath the trappings. I didn't realize that it was not only okay, but essential to own my viewpoints, feelings and perceptions if I truly wanted to be me. I found the courage to engage more fully in life, more as me, and happily, without the eating disorder."

Creating a synthetic personality, trying to fit into an increasingly unsettled and ever-changing culture with volatile values, Molly had found herself in huge confusion, one with a broken inner compass. There was safety in choosing a stereotype, a ready-made personality already acceptable to the people around Molly. She knew she'd fit in, but it was a shortcut and deep down she knew that. She also knew that at some point she'd have to do the hard work to figure out who she really was and what her true purposes were.

The thump in her soul served to remind her daily that she was not wholly herself and happy. She knew, perhaps more than most, what it felt like to have an unsettled inner life. Thus motivated, Molly worked hard to find herself and her inner compass again and to grow into the confident, healthy woman she is today; productive and valuable. Perhaps her story points us in the direction of the work that we all need to do, whatever our age or situation in life. We are invited to stop living behind the masks of stereotypes and personas. We are encouraged to not settle for substitutes and short-cuts. We need to do the work to find out who we really are and then muster the courage to bring to the world our own unique gifts.

Self-Examination is Tiring Work

We need to do the work and to be reminded that the work is exhausting. When Socrates says, "The unexamined life is not worth living," and that we are to, "know thyself," I think I understand what he means. However, as I look back over the years and layers, I am worn down by the thump which has seldom left me alone. If there's one thing the thump inspires, it is self-examination. The examined life can be incredibly tiring, especially when we go it alone. But still, we continue to long to be our truest and deepest selves, to dream of relationships where we can be unguarded, transparent, and fully loved. The rewards of a self-examined life can be huge, repaying all the hard work.

Conversations Reveal Who We Are to Ourselves and Others

Molly also said that her saving grace came through healing conversations. Healing conversations serve to help us find our truest and deepest identities. We learn about ourselves and our own hardwiring in meaningful conversation, where good questions are asked back and forth and where there is two–way safety and trust. We learn by being able to reveal ourselves in connection with others. We are liberated in being free to talk about our fears, thoughts, personal beliefs, preferences and our own transgressions. Such conversations are healing conversations in which we are truly turning together and turning toward truth.

If we can find out more about who we are in the safety of healing conversations, maybe we can express freely what we want and where we want to go. Maybe we can find what's missing from our lives.

It's so funny (strange) we don't talk any more.

Chapter 6

Relational Intimacy— The Missing Piece

The deepest way we have to share life, ideas, feelings and relationship is through meaningful conversations, whether written or spoken.

I have been privileged to perform hundreds of wedding ceremonies; big and small ones, simple ones and those for which I was thankful I was not paying the bills. About a year ago, I performed a ceremony at a very exclusive resort in Southern California. Everything about the wedding was beautiful, planned to the last detail and completely engaging. I worked with multiple wedding coordinators; the site coordinator, the day-of coordinator, the bride's personal assistant coordinator and the food and beverage coordinator.

The team hired to video the event consisted of six camer-apersons. They brought along enough equipment for a feature movie shoot: the drone overhead, two steady-cams and several fixed cameras. I wore three mics that day: one for video, one for audio, and one for backup.

This was a huge deal. I had worked with the bride and groom in the months leading up to the wedding. We had talked all about roles, expectations, responsibilities and the commitments that make marriages great. The bride and groom had been lovely, mature, engaged and committed to listening and learning.

They stood in an ideal setting. They each looked about as good as humanly possible. Family and friends sat on a cliff side overlooking the Pacific. They joined hands. They spoke the words, "I take you to be my wedded wife, to have and to hold from this day forward, for better for worse, for richer, for poorer, in sickness and in health…" My mind wandered. Do you think they really know what that means, "for better, for worse?"

A few days later I was enjoying lunch. Since I was paying, I chose Wendy's! As I sat down to eat, there was a commotion at the door. I turned to see a very petite woman wrestling a wheelchair. Before I could get up and help, she navigated the door and entered the dining room. She pushed the wheelchair to a seating area beside a television where she spun the wheel-chair around.

She reached into a bag and took out a cloth. She wiped the face of the man in the wheelchair she had pushed to the table. She leaned in and whispered to him. He smiled, spoke back. He was clearly her husband. He seemed to have suffered a stroke though both looked far too young to be dealing with such things. She made him comfortable then sat and they talked some more.

I watched him as she went away to order. He kept her in his line of sight. He was visibly relieved when she returned. When the food arrived, she carefully fed him. They chatted and each smiled and leaned into the other.

I remembered the words spoken in an almost perfect setting, "I take you… to have and to hold, from this day forward, for better, for worse, for richer, for poorer, in sickness and in health."

The couple in the restaurant was clearly living out the full implication of those vows. We all desire and pray that we can live into such sacred space. I pray it over every couple I marry and further all of the families I serve.

This is the heart of what we have lost. This is the deepest source of the thump. We have lost the intimate dance of connection. I watched other people around the room. No one else seemed to share in the same way. Here or there a couple smiled or perhaps exchanged a friendly sentence. Several argued, most seemed occupied with their phones but no one else seemed to be dancing. I think we all long for such deeply connected relationships.

What is connection? It is the many shared moments that bind us together. What is required to have such connection? Our stories connect us. Shared experiences connect us. Laughter connects us, but underneath all of that we deeply connect through attentiveness, kindness, tenderness, and compassion.

How do we understand the content of kindness, tenderness and compassion? We have to talk. The deepest way we have to share life, ideas, feelings and relationship is through meaning-ful conversations, whether written or spoken. The primary way we can learn, grow, connect, understand and become relation-ally involved is with our words. All our understanding is built through communication.

Talking at this deeper level is terrifying. Many of us have fallen into the habit of rigidly holding onto our own personal points of view. A deeper conversation would threaten to reveal these deeply held prejudices. Often, we would rather be right than connected. Clinging to our extreme or rehearsed views prevents deep, meaningful conversations. The longings of the people in these conversations get grievously ignored.

Healing conversations are not formal. They do not follow a prescribed template or patter, like a phone solicitation script. These conversations are alive, dynamic, surprising, and refresh-ing. Growth takes place and so does the joy of connecting; of letting life pass through your lips from your heart and soul and listening with deep concentration. Each moment is unique, custom made.

We see examples of poor communication all too often in life, in books and in movies and we scoff and say the word "dysfunc-tional" to allude to that situation. Why don't we connect with ease, spontaneity and deep joy with each other? We've touched on some barriers to great conversations in previous chapters. The right/wrong trap, extremism in our culture, hostile individu-als, and hiding within a tribe or behind a mask are some of these. Our personal brokenness and issues also get in the way.

Our fears, insecurities, and judgmental attitudes, adopting the habit of thinking in extremes or in generalities—all these things keep us apart. So, we do what we know, which is speak out of our own needs. That naturally causes us to push our own agendas which sabotages safe communication and banishes intimacy. We subtly send the message that the other person is wrong and that their opinion or thoughts don't matter.

If we experience too many interactions where our perspectives are pitted against another person's perspectives, we shut down, retreat, and don't try again. We walk away feeling empty and alone. This is especially true when the other person is self-absorbed and dramatizing the negativity of their issues instead of talking through them. Also, it is too dangerous to talk in those instances when the only acceptable outcome is to name the winner and the loser.

So, how do we overcome this and begin to engage in significant, relevant, engaging, life-building, energizing, fun conversations? After all, it takes at least two, and it's a process, not a singular, shining moment. (Though in healing conversations, you can expect several shining moments.) INTENTION & DESIRE

First, one needs to answer these questions. Do I really want this? Do I truly want to be seen, heard, known, and exposed at my deepest levels? Do I want to see into someone else's world? Do I want to experience their heart and soul up close and personal? Am I willing to give and not just receive?

My heart pounds a resounding "yes!" Why don't we unsettled people stand up and start a revolution where we celebrate the searching, longing and unsettledness of all the people in the world who may feel they don't fit in? The idea that we would raise up a group of people who are valued precisely because they are deeply committed to healthy processes would be a major shift in our cultural leanings. What if we were more willing to see a number of perspectives and committed to have fewer fixed answers? Not knowing is necessary to knowing. If we don't know that we don't know then how will we ever actually know? We could celebrate those who don't thrive on conflict, but who seek greater knowing. We could begin to listen to those who thrive on resolution, who wish to separate out from tribal wars where they had been too easily shouted down, or drowned out. We could invite our loved ones to find their voices. And, each of us could reverently seek to understand the power of words.

Chapter 7

Words

*Every thought of human existence is shared and
given life through words.*

The room's lighting is subdued. The tension is palpable. She sits drawn up in one corner of the couch. There is a tissue in one hand and she cries off and on. He sits in the other corner, defiant, weary, looking bewildered. He fluctuates from being soft and vulnerable to being angry and out of reach. They don't look at each other, but both look outward for affirmation and understanding. They feel hopeless, alone, misunderstood and wounded.

I have sat with such couples and groups for the last thirty years. Some have deep underlying issues and others are just living out the confusion that often accompanies relationships.

Most of them think they are locked into relationships that are fundamentally flawed and have little hope of being healed.

I am continuously amazed in those tension filled rooms of the power of words. Not just the words themselves, but the tone in which they are delivered, the body language that underwrites the conversations and the synergy that can tear down walls in a single, unsuspecting second or send the situation spiraling out of control. Words have power. We do not always use them wisely. Frederick Buechner speaks of this mystical power:

"The invisible manifests itself in the visible. I think of the alphabet, of letters literally—A, B, C, D, E, F, G, all twenty-six of them. I think of how poetry, history, the wisdom of the sages and the holiness of the saints, all of this invisible comes down to us dressed out in their visible, alphabetic drab. H and I and J, and K, L, M, N are the mold that our inner-most thoughts must be pressed into finally if we are to share them; O, P, Q, R, S, T, U is the wooden tongue that we must speak if we are ever to make ourselves known, that must be spoken to us if we are ever to know."[3]

Every thought of human existence is shared and given life through words. Every human longing and emotion is addressed and healed, or shattered, by these letters thrown together and delivered nicely-wrapped or carelessly thrown. They are received as unexpected gifts or as shrapnel posing deadly danger. It all depends on how they are arranged and how they are delivered.

---

3   From the *Alphabet of Grace* by Frederick Buechner, pg. 40. Harper Collins copyright 1970

Words are the building blocks of all our thoughts, ideas, and dreams. They are the foundation of knowledge and of all human interaction. Words are the currency that allows us into the marketplace of learning or teaching, loving and being loved, understanding and being understood. Still we too often treat them casually and thoughtlessly. The Holy Bible[4] offers us the ancient wisdom of James:

> **James 3:2–6a: 2** We all stumble in many ways. Anyone who is never at fault in what they say is perfect, able to keep their whole body in check. **3** When we put bits into the mouths of horses to make them obey us, we can turn the whole animal. **4** Or take ships as an example. Although they are so large and are driven by strong winds, they are steered by a very small rudder wherever the pilot wants to go. **5** Likewise, the tongue is a small part of the body, but it makes great boasts. Consider what a great forest is set on fire by a small spark. **6** The tongue also is a fire, a world of evil among the parts of the body. It corrupts the whole body, sets the whole course of one's life on fire…"

Building Blocks

Imagine the potential if we could create safe spaces in which people could be vulnerable, heal from past wounds and learn to engage in meaningful conversation? What if, with our words and patience, we could open closed hearts, build trust, and help people feel liberation and joy at the prospect of talking hon-

---

4

estly about their fears, thoughts, beliefs, hopes, and dreams? We could talk each other out of brokenness and isolation and into connection and wholeness. We could talk ourselves into some places in life that have yet to be built. We could talk ourselves into a renewed marriage, or a real understanding of our children. We could talk ourselves into politics that unite instead of divide. We could talk ourselves into a society that is fair and nurturing. We could talk ourselves into almost anything.

We could talk ourselves out of some things, too. We could talk ourselves out of anxiety or loneliness or depression. I am not saying we could use words to convince ourselves we are not anxious or lonely or depressed. I am saying we could use our words to build a bridge that allows us to move into connection with others and away from our lonely anxiety. We could use our words to bring light and hope to the inner parts of souls that are trapped in depression.

When I really stop to consider the concept, I am moved by the thought that words really are those powerful building blocks that are the basis of all human interaction. We ought to respect and honor these little arrangements of letters for the mystical powers they possess. We ought to learn to use them wisely.

Healing Conversations

So, what do you need in order for life to be more meaning-ful? A better marriage? A deeper sense of inner peace? A sense of reconciliation with issues in life, the culture and the world? Words have power and they can wound, but they can also heal. Words… can… heal. Think about that phrase for a second. Let it sink in.

POWER OF WORDS

We possess the powerful building blocks that can soothe a human soul. We already know how to form them and send them out into the world. We communicate every day. Our words are doing some work in the world. Are they healing words or diseased words? The Bible has a mystical understanding of words. The prophet Isaiah says:

> **Isaiah 55:10–11: 10** As the rain and the snow come down from heaven, and do not return to it without watering the earth and making it bud and flourish so that it yields seed for the sower and bread for the eater, **11** so is my word that goes out from my mouth: It will not return to me empty, but will accomplish what I desire and achieve the purpose for which I sent it.

Isaiah is reminding us that words don't just get spoken and then fade away. They keep on working and working and working. He is referring here to God's word, but the Bible understands that our words also have staying power. They are so powerful in fact, that the Bible teaches that we are accountable for our words, especially the ones we have spoken carelessly.

Don Miguel Ruiz, in his book *The Four Agreements,* says the first agreement is to "Be impeccable with your word." The word is the power you have to create. Your word is the gift that comes directly from God. The Gospel John writes about the creation and says, "In the beginning was the word and the word was from God and the word was God." Through words you express your creative power. It is through words that you manifest everything. What you dream, what you feel and what you really are, will all be manifested through words.

Words are challenging. People can be difficult; motives and trust, tricky. Many people are not safe, but somebody must take the first step of risk and choose to be both vulnerable and safe. I have sat with individuals, couples and groups over the last three decades and am continuously amazed in those tension-filled rooms of the power of words.

Not just the words themselves, but the intention behind them, the tone in which they are delivered, the body language that underwrites the conversations. I have seen impossible situations melt away as one person finds words from deep within and a sincerity born out of desperation that sets free some power that is a wonder to behold; a power that brings us together.

Remember the couple hugging separate corners of the couch in the example that opens this chapter? Imagine that husband finding a few words of appreciation, offering an awareness of his wife's needs and even a few words of admiration. I've seen such words spoken as tears spill down cheeks. I've watched bodies uncoil from dark lonely corners, the mood soften, and couples lean in, and reach toward each other. The miracle of healing conversations had begun.

What do you and I want? We want to love and be loved, to know and be known, and we want to be healed. What do we need to know to be able to bring these desires to life?

Chapter 8

Trust

*Since at our essence, there is no one like us, the
relationships that spring forth from two individuals
will be unique in expression and creativity.*

I've discovered that conversations can only really heal the participants if they have certain vital elements. Healing conversations are more art than science. Consciously, and with awareness, you choose what elements must be there to bring about meaning and fulfillment for the individual in front of you. Art is all about selection from a wide variety of things and choosing what communicates best and what effect you want to create. Science is more about formulas for observing or doing things. Curiosity and exploration are what drive both art and science, or what they both have in common and both are necessary to life. But, I want to emphasize that this book is not about adopting formulas, it is about principles, that when put into practice, these principles bring about very fresh, un-rehearsed and revitalizing communications.

The next few chapters highlight seven principles presented in a certain order because for me, these elements build on one another. Think of these elements as artist tools. As a visual artist, for example, you have canvases, paints, brush strokes, light, a model or subject, observation and inspiration. But those elements combine in a different way with each painting. It's the same in the art of communication, you have elements and tools. You have your awareness of the other person and your good intentions for a healing outcome. Let those intentions lift the person to whom you speak. Approach conversation in your own unique, fresh way—always considering the uniqueness of the other person. Any conversation can be made colorful and helpful using your imagination, inspiration, intuition and observation to guide you. I hope you will join me as we renew a commitment to revive the art of conversation in our lives and relationships. If we are committed to this art, I know it would be a better world!

The first of these elements is TRUST. The definition of trust is, "the firm belief in the reliability, truth, ability, or strength of someone or something." (English Oxford Living Dictionary). In this chapter I want to illustrate some aspects of building trust.

Daughters

I am the proud father of four beautiful daughters. Each daughter has her own unique personality, likes and dislikes, and outlook on life. It has been stunning to me how each one came with her own software already loaded. Each was hardwired with personality that, looking back, was already on display in labor and delivery. They were not blank slates on which to draw.

One thing all have shared in common, however, is my desire to keep them safe. When they were younger, I literally had nightmares about their physical safety. My wife and I worked hard to keep them strapped in, away from the edge of the pool, off the top of the cabinets and away from the stove. As they have grown up our fears have been more focused on their emotional safety.

In a conversation with one of my daughters recently, I launched into a random illustration and from that moment, the image has continued to grow in my mind. I think this image captures what I've learned about the first element of a healing conversation: trust. How do you build trust?

The Run of the Castle

Imagine that you have built yourself a castle. It's got a lot of space inside with a beautiful inner courtyard lit from skylights where natural light helps things grow. There are turrets providing lovely views. There are hallways paved with imaginative art you've created or obtained. Perhaps there are geraniums of many colors in window boxes. Your home offers a reasonable amount of security. Your dreams for the castle are to live in it with others in peace, security, tranquility and happiness. You have no desire to be alone in your castle, but you're smart enough to know that the peace and tranquility will be directly proportional to who is allowed inside.

As with any castle there are lines of defense and ways of entry for people you wish to let in. Each layer of defense has a specific purpose and each layer must be overcome in order to gain access to the castle. It's important to note that at each line of defense the process of allowing a person closer to the castle could end. The person is either recognized as a friend, misunderstandings are overcome and eliminated or the person is perceived as a threat and the threat is shut out. The process is designed to keep the people inside the castle safe and those who cause harm kept outside.

Each of us is really a castle of sorts. We are our own place of safety and refuge. We, too, have lines of defense. We want to keep people out who cause us harm and we want to welcome those who make the castle a warm and loving place of fulfillment, love and security. Over the years I wish I had seen this more plainly. I have been guilty of wishing someone would be the kind of friend who could have full run of the castle, only to find that they were not trustworthy with the inner workings of the castle.

I've watched my daughters allow a boy or two go past a line of defense in their hearts, only to be hurt and heartbroken. Seeing that is difficult for a dad. I don't think in all their growing up years I had the right words to help them understand how to defend their castles. I didn't have them because I had poor lines of defense myself. After some years, experience and thought, this castle idea has come to represent a meaningful image of trust building and at some basic level it begins in defending your castle. There is no doubt that trust building will also include getting out, risking, being proactive, and reaching out, but for a moment consider the lines of defense. I think it is very important to state clearly that the defenses of our castles are not primarily designed to keep people out. They are primarily designed to let the right people in.

The Moat

The moat is designed to keep the unknown visitor at a distance until he or she is vetted. Let a stranger come too close, too fast and our expectations may not match their intentions, abilities or values. An example of this comes from a couple I knew where the young man was charismatic, charming and swept the girl off her feet with his great communication and attention. She was so excited about the quick, deep connection, that she opened up, shared intimate feelings and viewpoints and therefore let him come very close to her. The boy continued this exciting, attentive behavior for a few weeks until they were "exclusively going out with each other" in other words, boyfriend and girlfriend. Then the boy, who had won the conquest, became more and more inattentive and hung out with his guy friends and began to take her for granted. The relationship became strained and tense. She had let him past the moat too quickly.

The moat forces a person to keep their distance so we can assess them. We can figure out if we will invite them to come closer. Ideally, from this distance they can't really hurt us. The first line of defense calls for some very simple questions:

1. Do you do what you say?
2. Are you reliable?
3. Are you consistent?

They are pretty simple questions. If a friend or a loved one does not do what they say, it is an indicator that they may not be the best choice for deeper friendship and healing conversations.

If they are not reliable, you can make yourself crazy with frustration, but, in reality, they have simply fallen to the first line of defense. In the example above, the young lady kept holding onto the tense relationship far longer than she should have, wondering what she'd done wrong, trying to correct her behavior and reshaping her personality and hoping their relationship would become what they had created in the first few weeks. She should have told him he was not reliable and consistent and she could be friends from a distance, but not be boyfriend and girlfriend. She could have liked him, been kind when their paths crossed and even cared about him.

So, the moat is there to create a boundary so that the person is not allowed to go too deeply into the castle. Are they consistent? Trust is built around these simple principles—delivering what you promise, doing what you say you will do, and not doing what you say you will not do. If someone is unpredictable in their responses, there will be a lack of safety and, therefore, a struggle to trust.

This first line of defense can help prevent the angst of this struggle. I want to say clearly that all defenses can stir up emotion because setting boundaries is not easy and having them set for you can be even worse. So, expect emotion. If someone says they'll call and they don't call, it's damaging. If they say they'll be there at a certain time and aren't, it's frustrating. If one day they are fully present, but the next day they aren't, it's unsafe.

These simple questions can help us diagnose what may be going wrong between you and those already in the castle.

And, they are useful in checking ourselves to see if *we* are doing what we say, being reliable, and being consistent.

I wish I could have said to my daughters, "No, that one didn't call when he said he would. Until he can do that, remember, he's (theoretically) not yet close enough to hurt you. Don't let him hurt you from the far side of the moat. That's why it's there!"

The Curtain Wall

Inside the moat is the curtain wall. More modern castles have a couple of these. They are walls around the whole complex so there can be a castle within the castle. The curtain wall is the second line of defense. There are three really important questions here:

Tender response to weakness.

1. Are you safe?
2. Do you want to know about me?
3. Or, are you preoccupied?

Does the person with whom you are building trust allow you to feel safe? Do they welcome your thoughts, weaknesses and fears? Do they want to know about you or is their primary interest in their issues, stresses and needs. As you have observed, good relationships inhale and exhale. Everyone gets time to open up about their pain, share their heart and be cared for by the other person. Do you find a natural, safe kind of give and take in the exchanges of conversations? Is there curiosity? Is there a sense of preoccupation on one person's part when you're together? Is something always a bit more important than you? This doesn't mean you can't be friends. This person is welcome to stand at the curtain wall any time, but that's where the level of trust exists right now. We have different expectations and levels of vulnerability at the curtain wall. We can sometimes be swayed because others have allowed the same people to have full run of their castles. That should not impact our decision to hold our ground. Holding our ground, no matter what others are doing, is the reason we have our own defenses.

This is about asking ourselves if there is any empty space. Does this person allow me space to be myself with no agenda, and nothing forced, just welcoming space? An empty, yet welcoming space invites my ideas and honors them. My ideas are as valuable as their ideas, my feelings are as important as their feelings. Neither is allowed to be the "advice and answer" person. If someone in a conversation is always the one with qualified answers, that can easily become unhealthy. Sometimes that leads to a feeling that we must accept their opinions and views or the friendship won't work. Such a lopsided relationship where one is more and the other less, can be stressful and not conducive to trust.

Trust is built over time through intentions manifested in genuine acts of love, grace, compassion and kindness. Intentions that remain in our heads and hearts do not build real trust in the tangible world. One of the biggest obstacles to overcome in trust building is the tendency in each of us to believe that our intentions are somehow bearing real results. I've talked to so many families in crisis where someone's idea of who they are and what they are bringing to the relationship exists only in their head. This is a simple process. Building trust involves real acts—ones that everyone sees and accepts as love, grace, compassion and kindness. Trust building doesn't happen in your head. It happens in the real world and it's visible.

To remind you of Henry Nouwen's powerful insight from his book, *Reaching Out...*

"Hospitality, therefore, means primarily the creation of a free space where the stranger can enter and become a friend instead of an enemy. Hospitality is not to change people, but to offer them space where change can take place."

People know when they have entered empty space. This kind of hospitality connects us. It creates very real feelings of peace, safety and connection. This kind of love and curiosity doesn't exist in someone's head, but in the real world. When such empty space exists, the curtain wall comes down and we invite people further into the castle. Don't forget that these lines of defense work for others, too. Asking ourselves these questions is at least as important as asking them of others. Healing conversations and the building of trust is always a two-way street. We must be as trustworthy as we are trusting.

The Drawbridge

If the first two lines of defense have been passed, then access to the castle is close at hand. How exciting it can be for the one seeking access. They see the multi-colored flags fluttering on the turrets, hear the music coming from the far reaches of the castle, beckoning. What will it be like inside? What beauty, adventures and treasures might be discovered? The drawbridge offers a line of defense that can be raised or lowered depending on the level of trust. At the drawbridge, three questions are really important:

1. Is there mutual vulnerability?
2. Is there willingness to risk?
3. Is there a willingness to meet needs and desires?

Before accessing the castle there is a need to establish mutual vulnerability. Even in relationships that have come this far, it is easy to find yourself the only one who is ever really risking anything. Conversational intimacy is built around this mutual willingness to be vulnerable and to risk being known. If both people are not willing to risk, it may mean this is a good place to hold. To lower the drawbridge and offer your own vulnerability without assessing the mutual risk voids the reason we have any defenses in the first place. There is so much to gain here. There is potential for deep, real life-giving friendship. The willingness to be vulnerable and to meet the needs and desires of the person with whom you are risking is the foundation of deep and lasting trust.

This space is right on the threshold of the castle and the potential for hurt is high. Each stage increases the vulnerability of both people and puts the castle at risk. Again remember, the defenses are not there so much to keep people out, but to be sure we are letting the right people in. These lines of defense are laid out as a means of assessing the nature of our relationships. These lines of defense are not drawn to critique or devalue someone. It's simply a way of more systematically building trust for both people. The person seeking entry into the castle wants to make sure he or she can handle what's needed and wanted by the one living in the castle and vice versa. With the drawbridge extended, we are left with just one more layer of defense.

The Grand Gate

Just before entrance to the castle comes the gatehouse. It is a tricky set of obstacles that serves as a last line of defense and offers a place of very real strength. The excitement mounts, the potential of rare friendship and relationship are palpable. What must the inner courtyard look like? Here the final three questions unfold:

1. Are you committed to this relationship?
2. What kind of relationship are you willing to create?
3. Are you willing to keep investing in the relationship?

Before entering the inner sanctum of the castle, I not only want to know if you are committed to this relationship, but also want to know what kind of relationship you are willing to create and keep creating. At this point we may not know the answers to all these questions, but we are comfortable talking about them. We ask good questions: Are you looking for the same kind of friendship as me? Do you want the same kind of depth, connection and involvement? Do we want to celebrate life in similar ways? And what are those ways? Do our goals and purposes in life align?

We need some time to think about this because this is where it gets very personal. This is not as much about your skills in relationships in general, but your real interest in our specific, unique relationship and your intentions and objectives in life as well.

This part is really about you and me at our deepest and highest selves. This is reaching toward another human being and creating a relationship like no other. It is about true intimacy in the middle of surrounding, nurturing trust. This intimacy may be a simple friendship, or it could evolve into a deeper romance. This kind of friendship lays a powerful foundation for a romance built on the relational intimacy of careful observation and mutual understanding. The connection is based on love, respect and excitement for each other's true identity. Wouldn't it be wonderful if all relationships were such custom-made, unique entities?

You are reliable. You do what you say and you're consistent, so come a little closer. You seem safe. You are curious about me and what goes on in my life, logistics and feelings. Come a little closer. When we talk you are fully present and not pre-occupied. Plus, you are willing to be mutually vulnerable and share in this risky proposition of conversation and relationship. Gladly, I invite you closer.

You may ask if this is possible in a broken world. Many of us are broken, but if we nurture our good intentions and practices and seek to overcome selfishness it can be done. Nurturing good practices and deleting negative ones is a huge task. It may take years of searching and costly counseling, but it is well worth it.

What If There's a Person in Your Castle That's Creating Chaos?

Sometimes we have let people into the castle only to find that our relationship is struggling. Perhaps, as we think through these defenses, we realize that someone in the castle is creating chaos. What do you do with people already in the castle who shouldn't be there? First, this is a book about healing conversations. Having the right words and ideas to speak to someone already in the castle is vital. Engaging in a conversation where there is clarity about the issues and about the desired outcomes is a great place to start cleaning up the castle. Second, it may be helpful to realize that although someone is already in the castle, it is not necessary that they have full run of the castle. You might consider limiting access to certain more sensitive areas in the castle, while working to heal the relationship. In short, it is never too late to pursue peace in the castle.

Building Trust

Lines of defense are vital to building real trust. They help us evaluate where we are in the process of relationship building and help us measure our own readiness to be a trustworthy partner in a relationship. These lines of defense also can help us see where we are hung up. In summary, regarding these lines of defense and acceptance, remember, **you are the castle**.

✦ The Moat is the first line of defense and there
    your questions are:
     1. Do you do what you say?
     2. Are you reliable?
     3. Are you consistent?

✦ **The Curtain Wall**, closer to the castle from
    the moat is the second line of defense and the
    questions are:
     1. Are you safe?
     2. Do you want to know about me?
     3. Or, are you preoccupied?

✦ **The Drawbridge** is the third line of defense.
    Here the questions are:
     1. Is there mutual vulnerability?
     2. Is there willingness to risk?

3. Is there a willingness to meet needs and desires?

✦ **The Grand Gate** is the last line of defense and this is where you ask these three questions:
   1. Are you committed to this relationship?
   2. What kind of relationship are you willing to create?
   3. Are you willing to keep investing in the relationship?

The questions that come with each line of defense need to be considered and answered honestly from the perspective of the unique personalities involved. Since at our essence, there is no one like us, the relationships that spring forth from two individuals will be unique in expression and creativity. Think about the people you love; each is irreplaceable, right? Remember that you are irreplaceable, too, and carry that conviction with you as you live, love and build healthy, trusting relationships. This all leads back to the reality that relationships are more art than science. And what do artists do? They practice their skills and use the very best tools.

Chapter 9

Humility

Healthy relational conversations grow out of a space that has been vacated by our own egos and agendas.

How do you know if you are Wise or Unwise?

You look at the fruit. Wise, mature people bear nourishing, sweet fruit—particularly in relationships. Unwise, immature people tend to bear fruit that is sour and distasteful. Fruit bearing shows up most vividly in relationships. If we are unwise, what do we do? We have to admit it.

However, an unwise person often denies personal responsibility for the problem, even if people around them are saying, "The way you talk to me hurts my feelings. I wish you wouldn't talk to me like that. I wish you wouldn't act like that."

And the response from an unwise person is, "Well, I'm not doing anything wrong!"

If you are wise, you distance yourself from this person until they gain some humility and growth! It's hard to practice wisdom around someone who is talking or acting in destructive ways. However, there is a cure for lack of wisdom. The cure is learning and practicing humility.

I Don't Know Much

Let's establish something right at the start. "I don't know much." That statement is a hard-fought-for and dearly-won truth about me. Don't think I am being self-effacing here, I don't think you know much either! I don't think the talking heads on television really know much. They can speculate for hours on end and can play with their predictions, but that's not knowledge. I don't think that most people, nowadays, who write popular books pretending to have THE answers know that much. When I read something that makes me come to life or hear someone talking that fully engages me, the words are seldom laced with absolutes and truisms. I am moved when someone gently talks with me about what they humbly believe as they process the complexities of life.

In my line of work I am called upon to speak every week. That requires scrutinizing an enormous amount of data. I'm more than thirty years into that process, but I knew in week one that I clearly didn't know much. Thirty years later, I feel even less confident about many more things. I'm okay with that admission. I have learned over time that my primary task is not to impart data and facts to people. My primary task is to share the journey with people; mine and theirs.

When that realization hit me, it changed my focus in speaking and my outlook on life. My calling became to share with my congregation what I am learning. That involved sharing my struggles and weaknesses and there is no scarcity of material that I have to draw from! Overall, it is a process of self-revelation. That leads me into a "fear and trembling" kind of space, week after week. Writing and delivering sermons is very vulnerable space for me. It necessitates confessing that I simply don't know much. However, that admission does not prevent me from deeply and passionately believing some things.

I walked into my office this morning and set it up for writing. I have some rituals around this. The desk has to be relatively clean. The lights are out except for my study lamps. I always light a candle because it just makes the room feel better. My computer plays the sounds of thunderstorms which is both soothing and blocks the outside activity of the office. My personality wants to engage with whoever is walking through the office. Quieting down and settling is a discipline. The Quakers call it "centering down."

Sometimes I sneak a look at the news and quickly run through a few Facebook notifications, telling myself it's important to know what's going on in the world. But, that's a mistake! I shouldn't do those things during my writing cocooning—the whiplash is instantaneous. My attempt to quiet the environment, to settle my inner self, is immediately blown apart by the voices, spins, rants, raves and absolutes of a thousand personal opinions. My senses are bombarded by politics, health problems, social issues, people in need, and to crises of all shapes and sizes. I am exposed, vulnerable and suddenly unsettled. I find myself arguing internally. A few more reads and I am seething at the illogical and unfair presentation of ideas and thoughts. Disappointment begins to fill my mind and eventually makes its way to my heart and I am saddened by shallowness. I've nearly ruined the time where I should invite inspiration to partner with me. I should know better.

Noting once again the bludgeoning effect of the news, I do remind myself that I don't know much and neither do the people who are talking, writing, posting, reacting and responding. In my humble opinion, the world would be a better place if we started every conversation with this confession. Of course, you wouldn't sell as many books or get invited to be interviewed, or get many likes on your posts, if you made this admission up front.

So, once again, I resolve to get quiet and feel my feelings, allow the peace and creativity to join me. When quiet, I am aware that the spaces that beckon to me are places that are filled with humility. Places where the people involved are gentle, kind, thoughtful, and as eager to learn as they are to share their own journeys. I could sit in those spaces and talk and share and be vulnerable and learn and grow all day long.

The admission that we don't know much is at the very heart of humility. The wise ones have been propagating the value of humility for a long time. We've been told over and over that this is the foundation of all things virtuous and relational.

"Humility is the solid foundation of all virtues." – Confucius

"Do you wish to rise? Begin by descending. You plan a tower that will pierce the clouds? Lay first the foundation of humility." –Saint Augustine

Assuming my working definition that, "We don't know much," may be inadequate to explain the intricacies of the concept, I give you this simple statement from Rick Warren:

"Humility is not thinking less of yourself, it's thinking of yourself less."

Simple, right? But it is so difficult to do. I believe that real communication must somehow be rooted in thinking of ourselves less. Few of us would ever open our mouths except to pursue an agenda, a goal, an outcome that we have in mind already. We have decided. We have determined our need and the desired outcome and even a strategy for reaching our goals. What other reason is there to talk? And therein lies a big trap, the trap of self-centeredness that will forever keep one from really touching another's soul.

Remember the three general purposes for talking? They are functional, sharing information and logistical issues. Let me be clear, though functional talking is basic, "When are we leaving?" "What's for dinner?" it still requires attentiveness and an effort to be effective. Then there is talking to promote an agenda, this could be forwarding a cause, but it could also mean one person trying to persuade the other. Both these levels of communication are greatly impacted by humility.

The third kind of talking is relational conversation, characterized by true hospitality and great listening skills. If humility and good listening skills are vital to effectively communicating functionally, then it is imperative to use these skills if we ever hope to communicate relationally. If we feel we are missing out on meaningful relational conversations, it might be fair to start by asking, "How often do we think of ourselves less and put our attention fully on another person?" Healthy relational conversations grow out of space that has been vacated by our own egos, perspectives and agendas. Not that these things are not useful, they have their place, but they are limited especially when we consider the enormous capacity each of us has for creativity. Humility matters because it forces us to get out of our own heads and into a space where we can connect with others. Saint Paul said it this way:

> **Philippians 2:3,** "Do nothing out of selfish ambition or vain conceit, but in humility consider others better than yourselves."

Humility means I am learning to engage with others without making myself the center of attention. This goes against some of our most basic instincts. We enter conversation so that we can feel connected and cared for, and to give another the comfort of knowing they are cared for. To think that we need to approach communication by putting others first can seem counterintuitive. However, learning the art of humility in conversation leads us toward healing conversations and those lead us toward healthy relationships. We do not reach our goal of healthy life-giving and mutually satisfying relationships by putting ourselves first.

Jesus said, "Whoever wants to be greatest among you should be the servant of all."

Humility changes the fundamentals about how I think about and enter conversations with others. There is always a danger here. A lack of humility and/or insecurity sometimes leads people to impose formulas on people, formulas they claim work every time. This is especially off-putting when the person imposing these formulae has a "know best" attitude. You know that person, they've just read a book or taken a course and they are practicing on you! But you really don't feel they are real or that they are really addressing you. If we become people more interested in producing correct-by-the-formula conversations than getting connected to people in a meaningful way, it will feel unnatural. When we do those things, our words can feel artificial. A truly humble conversation is not artificial in any way. The very opposite is true. It is the basis of getting back to very real connections.

> **"Pride makes us artificial and humility makes us real."** –Thomas Merton

Humility is the virtue that allows us to be open to others and vulnerable ourselves.

Knowing and Believing

Over the years I have heard a lot of "wisdom." I have been to lots of conferences. I've sat through endless meetings. The number of conversations one-on-one must number into the hundreds of thousands at this point. I can't prove it, but I think, practically speaking, humility comes down to recognizing the difference between what we know and what we believe. Let's go back to where we started, "I don't know much." Remember, that I don't think anyone else knows much either. I think our sense of knowing, being right and not needing to learn anymore on that particular subject, damages our ability to practice humility. When we communicate from that perspective, we carry a great deal of prejudice into our conversations.

And we see these prejudices on blogs, on TV, on the internet and on social media. That is the basis of a lot of our communication. The mentality of thinking we know all the answers is at the center of the "News as entertainment" movement. It is divisive and drives us to listen to people who speak what we already believe. Analysis, fact gathering, impartial reporting, and objectivity have given way to criticism, second guessing and pontificating. Let's be honest. The talking heads on television, the pollsters, the writers who fill up articles day after day and week after week, the analysts who comb through the aftermath of every event, speech and story do not *know* much. They may passionately believe some things, but they don't know.

Those educated, highly trained, and very often insightful people don't know how to fix the economy. Neither do you or I. They don't know how to repair the social issues that threaten to tear apart the unity of our culture. Neither do you or I. You get the idea. What is shocking is how often we act like we do. It is the height of arrogance and at the root of our inability to have real conversations. If I believe that I know how to fix the world, you can be sure that I will need to convince you and that will not be a conversation rooted in humility. If I believe that I am the smarter person in this conversation, it will not be rooted in humility!

Let's get personal. We are all starting from the same point of not knowing. It doesn't mean we do not have some good ideas or some passionate beliefs about how to fix relationships. It does mean that we are starting the conversation with the humble admission that we are equals in this conversation. I am not here to convince you or defeat you or out-talk you. I am here to share my viewpoints and I want to hear your viewpoints. I am here to understand what you believe and why you believe it. I am praying that you desire to understand what I believe and why I believe it. Since I don't know and you don't know, my beliefs might be persuaded to change based on our real and humble conversation.

Most of us carry in us pieces of very real and valuable truth in our stories and perspectives. Humility means I no longer label people in order to write off their values and beliefs. I want to stay away from conservative and liberal, or progressive, or Democrat, or Republican, or Christian, or Muslim because (and be honest here) those are too often just prejudicial ways of writing off whole groups of human beings as irrelevant. Instead, humility demands that we see others as holders of truth and information that could, when impacting our jumbled thoughts and beliefs, produce new understanding that none of us could have discovered alone.

Do you have the courage to admit out loud what you do not know? You may passionately believe some things, but please allow that these things are beliefs not knowledge.

1st Corinthians 8:1, Saint Paul said, **"Knowledge puffs up, but love builds up."**

Believe with all your heart, but don't let your beliefs shut out the very real thoughts, feelings and beliefs of those around you. Humility enables us to hear another, touch another, learn from another, find joy in another and to share of ourselves what another can hear, have and find meaningful. Humility is a skill that must be nurtured, refined and implemented if we are committed to healing conversations. Without it we hardly dare venture into the next skill of healing conversations. The very risky art of self-disclosure.

Chapter 10

Self-Disclosure

*Each of us is the leading expert on only
one subject: our life!*

The Secret of Great Public Speaking

A few years ago, I had the privilege of hearing Benjamin Zander speak. He had just written *The Art of Possibility* and was addressing many of its ideas. At the outset of his talk he informed us that he would be speaking for two hours. *That's a dangerous thing for a speaker to say,* I thought and anticipated a long afternoon. Two hours later, I was praying that he would give us a little more of his time, energy and insight. He was that good.

It made me realize the powerful nature of words and the art of offering them creatively. As a public speaker, it has been my lifelong commitment to master and refine the art. There are no scientific formulas by which we can guarantee engaging conversations. As I have observed earlier, it is much more art than science and no two people on the planet can be exactly alike. With that said, however, there are common values practiced by truly gifted speakers.

By the time I was sixteen years old, I knew I was going to spend my life as a public speaker. I felt sure my life was headed into a life in ministry which involved much public speaking. There was very little I understood about what that meant, but more than forty years later, it is still my first love. Whatever my misconceptions, I did understand that the art of public speaking would be a lifelong pursuit. Somehow, I knew that the only way to improve was to practice. I found myself beginning to think differently—the thoughts in my head needed to be organized into some meaningful outline. I started to form strong opinions about what a good speaker looked and sounded like. Without knowing much of anything about the art of public speaking I was becoming highly opinionated!

One of my first and most lasting impressions about public speaking happened one night when a group of us were sharing personal stories in a worship service. My thoughts were coming together in a calculated way. I rehearsed the outline in my head and when it came my turn to talk, I clicked through the points one by one, paying attention to the transitions and the logical flow of my thoughts. Upon the conclusion of my well-ordered monologue, a close friend of mine offered his story. His thoughts were rather disorganized, rambling, disconnected, hard to follow and yet, completely transformational.

Even though his story was not one of organized thoughts, they contained something that my reasoned-out comments had failed to include. In fact, I realized in that moment that most of us carefully avoid the one ingredient that allows our words to be meaningful—self-disclosure. My friend had innocently blurted out the raw truth about himself. I had sanitized my words so they would be once removed from my own vulnerability. I didn't want any of my profound thoughts to be reversed engineered into some deeper appraisal about who I was as a human being.

Years later, Benjamin Zander left me begging for more because he disclosed truths about himself and brought me along on his journey. I felt I knew him and his wife and how they talked privately and what they most valued. I felt I understood their vision, passion and goals for life. This was not a talk about a topic; this was a talk about life.

The most engaging speakers I hear are those who effectively practice self-disclosure with all its vulnerabilities. They are willing and creative in telling the truth about themselves. Of course, this is not a book about public speaking, it's about healing conversations, but what is true for an audience of many is deeply true of an audience of one. Self-disclosure is vital to meaningful and healing conversations.

You Are the Best Expert on One Subject

If humility is finally being able to admit how little we know, then it is easy to think we have very little to share. It is only logical that if I do not possess a lot of useful knowledge, I don't have anything of real value to offer. In a culture driven by experts it is easy to believe we must specialize in order to contribute.

Nothing could be further from the truth. Each of us is the leading expert on one subject, our life. That life is part emotions, part experiences, part mental gymnastics, part soul-searching and probably some combination of spirituality, angst, brilliant insight, insecurity, confusion and clarity.

Of all the topics we could choose to discuss, the most vulnerable is talking about ourselves—our true selves. And I'm not talking about self-centered narcissists who have not grown up and who cannot even see another person, let alone their points of view. I'm talking about you and me and the only topic we know so intimately. It is also one of the most meaningful contributions we can make to the people we love.

I am also not talking about a conversation that is a carefully constructed and rehearsed speech. That is part of a facade we put up when we are insecure and it is often our default setting in conversations. I am talking about conversations that might be disorganized, rambling, disconnected, and hard to follow and yet, because of self-disclosure are completely transformational! That kind of revelation is gold in any story we love to read or view on the screen. When we hear it in a personal conversation and attempt it ourselves, we are in a space that is vulnerable and risky, but immensely valuable.

Sacred Ground

I see a steady stream of couples preparing for marriage. For every couple who choose to have me conduct their ceremony, there is a mandatory counseling commitment. It kicks off every spring and fall with a pre-marital class. All the couples gather for group sessions and we talk about relationships. Eventually each couple meets with a private counselor as we work to prepare them for the challenge of a fulfilling marriage.

Every class features a section on communication. Just engaging in meaningful conversation is much more of a challenge than we have ever imagined. It is almost tiresome to introduce to those couples the old idea that the finest communication we can offer begins with "I" statements. "I think, I feel, I want, I like, I don't like," are perfect entrées into real conversation. They are also the most difficult. "I" language is incredibly important. It signals that someone is willing to talk about who they are and what is rolling around in that head of theirs.

There's no doubt that "I" conversations may start out rather shallow. "I like ice cream," is hardly a life changing revelation, still, it is a place to start. With each of our groups of couples I try to pour into them that "I" language is sacred space. It should trigger a kind of reverence in us. There should be a hush that falls on our busy thoughts and emotions, "Shhhh, someone is about to self-disclose." Maybe we should take off our shoes, this is holy ground! Someone is on the fire walk of self-disclosure. The slightest offering should be met with honor and encouragement. The best response when we hear the sacred word "I" is to ask clarifying questions. "Tell me more about that." "What was that like for you?" "When did you first realize that you liked ice cream?"

"Well, when I think about it, I really started to like ice cream at my Grandparents house." "What happened at their house?" "Well, every birthday that fell in warm weather and pretty much any July 4th, my whole great big extended family would meet at my grandparents' place. We called it, 'The Ranch.' The women would mix up their ice cream concoctions and pour them into ice cream freezers. The men would load those freezers down with ice and rock salt. Us kids would get a towel and take turns sitting on the freezers while they were hand cranked until the ice cream froze." "How does that make you feel?" "It reminds me of all those good years growing up. My grandparents are both gone. My dad, too. I live across the country and don't see much of my family, but ice cream reminds me. Yep, I do like ice cream!"

When was the last time you gave yourself 100% to listening to another human being? What would that look like? What does getting reverent actually mean? It means putting down the cell phone, switching off all thoughts about you and focusing on the other person. It means entering fully into the present moment, giving gentle eye contact and inviting body language. It means actively listening and drawing them out. It's about caring for the other person—turning on sympathy, empathy, and compassion. That means you have to first turn off judging—an important prerequisite. And it means you follow their train of thought and ask clarifying questions if you need to. It is sacred ground.

Given the space, time and attention, most people really want to self-disclose. I repeat this several times in this book because I believe each of us has a deep need to know and be fully known. The Apostle Paul in his great chapter on love, 1st Corinthians 13, hints that we want to know as we are fully known. Evidently, Paul believed that love has something intimately to do with being known. Love, worth, healing, and safety are joined around our ability to reveal ourselves and to have someone else take the risk of revealing themselves to us and to find in that vulnerability the security of being accepted and loved for who we really are.

COMPASSIONATE WITNESS

In a healthy relationship, partners move through this dance of "I" statements and clarifying questions and then transition to trading places. Roles reverse and the questioner becomes the focal point. They stammer out, "I think, I feel, I want," statements and their words are revered for their vulnerable self-disclosure. Those stumbling steps are met with encouraging questions as a loving partner leans in and listens closely for the secret inner workings of another's soul. This is sacred ground.

Just one word of warning, some of us are wired to listen and ask good clarifying questions. Some of us have learned to *only* ask clarifying questions and to seek to understand others. For some it has become a form of hiding in plain sight. We seek to understand others and keep the focus elsewhere. As long as the other person is talking about themselves, we are not at risk. That reticence to share may be because of shame or hurt. It may be because deep down we don't believe that anyone really cares about us and it's much safer to listen and make others feel valued than risk self-disclosure and be rejected or ignored. While we can't control everything, a healthy relationship inhales and exhales. We take turns disclosing and listening. If someone is not truly interested in the deeper, vulnerable parts of your inner world, then there will be a limit to how effective and connected a conversation can be.

The Heart of the Issue

When I am unencumbered by a need to prove my point, I am free to explore a new kind of conversation. I am free to engage in the one thing on which I have the authority to speak, me! No one else on earth knows as much about me as I do. No one else can tell me how I feel or what I think or define my inner world. I am the only person who has walked this inner sanctum. I am the only one who has ventured into the basement and under the floorboards. No one else knows as well as I do what's under the bed or in the closets or what is most deeply hidden. I am the expert.

My gut reaction to this truth is that no one else on earth cares to know. There are so many things about me that I don't even want to know, or to remember. So many experiences hidden in secret places trigger painful humiliations and sometimes hopelessness. There are things in this inner world that really haunt and hurt and drag up buckets full of shame. For many of us there are places in our inner world we no longer dare to visit. We ask, "How can my inner world be of any value?" There is the heart of the issue. We do not understand the true value that we have to offer. In my experience, where we are most vulnerable, is where we are most valuable.

As a culture we have all but lost the art of healing conversations. We have too often falsely believed that meaningful connection is about knowledge, skills, perfection and performance. Since we have been taught that our worth comes from performance, we spend a lot of time explaining our life. We spend time explaining what we were thinking and why we were thinking it and how that led to the choices we made. Usually when we are explaining those complex thought processes, we are protective, working to justify what we gained from our loss, and fortifying ourselves for what we are sure will be a critique.

How we think and the conclusions we come to are often illogical and silly to someone else. We often end up in a conversation about how we might have thought differently and reached different conclusions and how that might have led to a better outcome. All of which is, at some level hypothetical, frustrating and irrelevant. What we learn from our past choices might be a very meaningful, transformational and healing topic of conversation, but few of us feel safe enough to just talk plainly about such things. To do so involves being honest about how we've failed and how often we've felt foolish in the process. We don't feel safe enough with many people to admit such vulnerable areas of our inner world. So, instead, we spend time and energy trying to explain ourselves and to justify our behaviors. We harp on what we think we know. We explain life even though down deep we believe that much in life is inexplicable.

So, if it's not our knowledge and if it's not our explanations of life and its meaning that is so valuable, then what of true value do we have to share? We have ourselves to share. We have our own story to share. We have our own experiences to share. We have feelings and thoughts to share. Life may defy explanation, neatness, and conclusions, but the meaty vulnerability of human experiences is perfect for sharing.

Life sharing is only possible if we are willing to disclose ourselves. What we have to share is of untold and unknown worth. It is hidden inside every single sacred statement that begins with, "I think, I feel, I want, I like, I don't like…" Those simple baby steps lead us toward moments when we can begin to talk about our truest feelings, experiences, hurts, and failures. They open us up to speak about deeper things, the things we want or need or dream about. They are the launching points for conversations about how we experience life. It is the riskiest kind of communication and it is sacred. When someone utters an "I" statement around us it is the signal to quiet down and get reverent. Take off your shoes. This is holy ground.

At Seventeen

In 1973, a twenty-two-year-old aspiring artist named Janis Ian came across a newspaper article that highlighted a young woman's journey into adulthood. It was a discussion about how high school popularity didn't carry over into anything meaningful in later life. In that article the young girl was quoted as saying, "I learned the truth at eighteen." Janis Ian was jolted by that sentence. She had already released seven albums and written many songs, but those words triggered something very personal in her. She began to write an autobiographical song around that single sentence. When the song was completed, she had no intention of recording it or even letting others read it. It was intensely personal and self-revealing. She altered the phrase to read, "I learned the truth at seventeen," and began to realize that perhaps her experience was not the exception, but the rule. Most of us are familiar with the haunting lyrics. When Ian wrote and recorded this autobiographical piece of self-disclosure, she offered the truth about her life and feelings. As is almost always the case, that truth was met with the astonishing gift of identification. The proof of this identification is that, "At Seventeen" won Janis a Grammy and sold over a million copies by the end of 2004. Critics eventually came to consider "At Seventeen" Janis Ian's signature song.

So many times we say to ourselves upon hearing someone else's disclosure, "I feel that way too, but I thought I was the only one." I have rarely seen any effort at genuine self-disclosure that is not met with this incredibly redemptive truth: "me too!" That is the heart of the matter. My most valuable asset is my story and it is yours, too. Healing conversations are built on self-disclosure, and they go deeper and higher when you add true curiosity.

SELF-DISCLOSE LEADS TO → "ME TOO"

Chapter 11

Curiosity

> *"Sometimes recognizing and acknowledging this need for someone to be curious about us brings deep clarity to some inner longing that is going unmet."*

Let It Out

In 2007, Kimberly Clark, the parent company of Kleenex brand tissues launched an advertising campaign entitled, "Let it out." It featured a bright blue couch sitting in the middle of urban chaos. Next to the couch was an end table with a box of Kleenex and a chair. A man appeared in the commercials and invited random people to sit down and "let it out." What follows is amazing. People consented to sit down and share their stories—any story at all. They told stories about life; good things, sad things, hard things and fun things. Very few got through their sharing without real and cathartic tears. Their brief moments of sharing were followed by heartfelt embraces and other signs of real relational connection between people who were strangers just minutes before.

We are deep and mysterious beings. We are capable of carrying within us, every kind of emotion at once. We can feel great joy and deep sadness all at once. We can feel inspiration and depression in a single breath. Our minds run on without much supervision and even manage to surprise us when we stop long enough to give attention to our deeper, personal thoughts. The complex mysteries that inhabit the secret places of our inner worlds are so intricate that there is a genuine need for us to explore there. Perhaps the greatest adventure is the adventure inward.

While the content of that inner world is a complex labyrinth of tunnels, canyons and caves, some of the means by which we explore that world are simple. Words have the ability to bring light, understanding and peace. The right words can begin to sketch out a usable map that allows us to navigate our inner world with ever-increasing ease and confidence. Healing conversations only happen between people who have come to understand the gift and power of words which can transform inner worlds from dark places of mystery and anxiety to peaceful places of refuge and strength. They happen to people who are willing to humbly confess that they don't know much, who are willing to risk themselves in self-disclosure, who understand such vulnerability in others as sacred ground and who offer the gift of curiosity.

I am continually amazed by the power of simply being curious about another person's story. Strangers sitting on a couch in the middle of a sidewalk, weep, laugh and jump for joy because a stranger asks them to talk about their lives. Every day, millions of people walk into the offices of therapists who grant them the gift of their undivided attention, a genuine desire to understand, and skilled questions filled with curiosity. Therapists don't talk a lot. They create space for others to talk and practice the art of good, on-point and probing questions.

In my experience in therapy, I found those hours some of the most sacred in my life. Long before answers could be wrestled out of my complex inner world, I found healing in being heard. I looked forward most weeks to the hour I would spend being the entire topic of conversation. I knew I would be asked questions about a subject I longed to know more about, me! I was never naive about the fact that I was paying someone to do this work, but skilled therapists know how to care. For one hour no one needed something from me. Someone was simply curious about me, my story, my feelings, my view of life and the world.

I have friends like that. They are attentive people. They are the ones who say, "How are you?" And if a person gives a glib answer, they look you straight in the eyes and say, "How are you, *really*?" These friends can sit down in that conversation and remember what you told them last week, last year or a remark you made in passing. They ask good questions and laugh with you and get mad when you get mad and speak words that help untangle the knot in your gut. They often do it with no special knowledge or deep insight or advice drawn from personal experience. They do it by offering one of the rarest gifts on earth, their curiosity.

By now most of you reading this are likely thinking about how much you need someone like that in your life. Any time my mind ventures into this track, I find myself longing for more people who might be genuinely curious about me. The need is genuine and real. We all need that, but we also strive to be that. Sometimes recognizing and acknowledging this need for someone to be curious about us brings deep clarity to some inner longing that is going unmet. There is clarity in finding words to describe our deeper needs, but the insight is also a call to become more curious. As people committed to practice the fine art of healing conversations, we are not just looking to find curious people, we are looking to become curious people.

Are You Interested?

Let me ask a crucial question, "Are you interested in other people?" Being curious is not about pretending to be interested in others. Being curious grows out of a very real belief about others; that they are worth knowing. Selfishness is the enemy of meaningful relationships. It is the enemy of healthy communication. This is the paradox of curiosity. We see the value of curiosity because we want to talk about ourselves, but we can only be truly curious about others if we can put our needs in the appropriate context.

Ego-centric people rarely experience true curiosity because they are full of themselves. They have no room in their inner world for empathy because their own hurt, need and anxiety fills up every conversation. Constantly telling our own story and our own experiences pushes aside the gentle art of curiosity. Dominating conversations, talking too much, giving too many details, and failing to let others find their way into the conversation, are all indicators that we are just not that interested in the people around us. Let me say that I recognize some of the irony of where we are.

We just spent time and energy talking about the need for self-disclosure and now I am saying we ought to talk less and listen more. If that feels like a contradiction, let me highlight two things. One, self-disclosure is a very specific, vulnerable, sacred kind of self-sharing. It is not just a lot of haphazard talking about ourselves. So much of our talking about ourselves does not rise to the level of self-disclosure but lingers far below at a level of logistics or even trivia. Second, all conversation is about balance. Even in sacred self-disclosure, the "I" speaker and the clarifying questioner, should willingly trade roles back and forth. So, curiosity and self-disclosure become a part of the sacred, back and forth dance of healing conversations.

Leaning In

Curiosity is the art of leaning into those precious moments of self-disclosure. Leaning in means I quiet my own mind and focus my attention. Something in my spirit has shifted and I genuinely long to know and understand. Something in me knows that this is another human being's vulnerable, self-disclosure and curiosity is the attitude that provides a ready and immediate sanctuary. Curiosity creates a deep sense of safety.

The art of curiosity engages us in active listening. We inherently know the difference between courtesy and active listening. Courtesy may listen with the ears, but curiosity actively listens. It listens with ears and heart and mind. Words are processed.

Emotions are evaluated and soaked up. Empathy is shared. The mind engages. It stays present in the moment refusing to wander ahead or away.

The body gets involved too. We send all the nonverbal cues that we are actively engaged. We make eye contact. We acknowledge what's being said. We respond appropriately. We lean in, literally. At times we might have to hold a hand or touch a shoulder. Without curiosity engaging us in active listening we will have no idea how the conversation should proceed. Too often conversations are interrupted by someone pushing. We push to offer our opinions. We push because we want to correct some misinformation. We push because we are looking for a predetermined outcome. Those things must not interrupt the curiosity. If they are allowed to interrupt, it means our curiosity was not very deep or strong. We are longing to understand what is being felt, experienced, and described by a fellow human being. Curiosity has one goal and that is to learn.

Feeling and Fact Finding

Curiosity is all about exploring the facts and feelings of another human being. It asks good, thoughtful questions that draw out more and deeper parts of another person's story. People tend to reveal the simplest things and see how they are received. If we prove we are interested and provide a safe place for self-disclosure, others will open up more and more. Nothing is more honoring than a person who shows genuine interest in the unfolding of our sometimes disorganized stories.

The curious are gathering details and working to understand how this story came together and how it helped shape this human being. However, curiosity is not just about being interested in the facts of the story. When we focus on facts alone, we tend to dispute, correct, defend or even get lost in the narrative. We might be much more interested in the feelings that are being experienced. However, most of us tend to be terrified of other people's feelings, especially negative ones.

For years I've watched couples in counseling fight over whose feelings are valid. I've watched terrified men overflowing with frustration try to silence their wives as unchecked feelings flood the room. Most of us have a hard time putting meaningful words to our feelings. We have gotten used to trying to edit our feelings for accuracy and propriety. Feelings are not good or bad, true or false, right or wrong, but they are real. Feelings are feelings.

Curiosity demands that I be willing to hear feelings. Someone expressing their feelings is not a threat or an accusation, but a window to their soul. Feelings are often jumbled up and tangled together and most of us don't know which ones are closer to the truth about us and which ones come from another planet. When someone has the grace to be curious about our feelings and helps us draw them out into the open, our feelings are no longer invisible.

If the listener continues to have the grace to lean into our feelings and understand the pain we experience, or the confusion, or the joy; we find ourselves suddenly engaged in the deepest and most healing kind of conversation. Further, when given this kind of freedom to express ourselves, most people find the clarity to self-regulate. I've seen deep, heartfelt apologies come out of these cathartic moments and no one had to prompt, control or seek those moments of reconciliation. The very act of being curious and patient as the feelings tumble out laid the groundwork for healing. Most of us long to be seen, heard and understood and curiosity is the means by which we receive and offer that gift to others.

Understanding

This process of being truly interested, leaning in, actively listening, and drawing out facts and feelings, offers the hope of doing something that is extremely rare in relationships. It offers us the chance to understand another human being. Often when we can truly understand someone else's perspective, we find that conflict no longer exists. Or, if it does, we can see the path toward reconciliation much more clearly. It takes great patience to be a person of curiosity, but in relational terms this is powerful medicine. It also takes commitment. Curiosity is an art, but it is also a skill. The skill must be learned, practiced and improved. In working the skill, we become open to the artful use of the skill. It is easy to think of curiosity as a talent that we either possess naturally or we don't. Some people are much more inclined to be naturally curious, but all of us have the ability to grow in the practice of curiosity.

What is true of individuals is also true of groups of people. When people of different political persuasions can sit down in humility, become vulnerable in self-disclosure and practice real curiosity about the opposing perspectives, powerful understanding can begin to grow even in the most diverse belief structures. This holds true for religion, sports, lifestyles, cultures and traditions. There is strength in diversity, but only if the diversity finds meaningful ways to connect. Curiosity about how others see and experience life offers the hope of real connection. Saint Francis is credited with these famous lines:

> O Divine Master, Grant that I may not so much seek
>> To be consoled as to console;
>> To be understood as to understand;
>> Curiosity is a sacred gift that leads us toward the
>> hope of understanding others.

Chapter 12

Respect

Respect demands much more than tolerance

Subjectivity

Years ago, I was invited to teach a class for the local community college. They host a "Life Skills" department that is designed for senior adults. The teacher who had been leading the World Religions class was moving away and they heard I was somehow involved in religion and thought I might be a match. The fact that the college had begun to rent our facility for classes might have had something to do with it too. I thought it would be a fun challenge and committed to the task. I read and studied and prepared a semester's worth of lectures on world religions. Fall arrived and my class was actually full.

Forty adults with intimidating resumes of educational accomplishments gathered for our exploration. They were lifelong educators, engineers, professionals from almost every walk of life. They were philosophers, dreamers and sages. Most had a post-graduate degree and a lifetime of experience. I realized at once that I was in over my head. As the class began and I launched into my first lecture, a hand went up. I responded and accepted my first question of my new teaching career: "Since you are a Christian minister, how do you propose to teach this class with any objectivity at all?"

That's a really good first question. From a philosophical perspective it could be asked this way, "How do you plan to emerge from your own subjectivity and offer something more than slanted, tainted, and prejudiced information?"

I wasn't sure how to satisfactorily answer the question. The one thing that you can hardly ever escape is your own subjectivity. Wherever you go, there you are. In the moment, I remembered a simple thought that had occurred to me when I first started in ministry and said that. "I will commit to you and to this class that I will always be fair. I will be fair to the material. I will be fair to the perspectives of other religions. I will not make fun of anyone or anything. I will not be a critic. I will be a student with each of you as we commit to learn what world religions teach and believe. If, at any point you feel I am not being fair, I invite you to call me out and hold me accountable."

I taught that group for the next five years, through three more iterations of world religions and philosophy classes. We had a great time. We were as diverse in our backgrounds and beliefs as you could possibly imagine. Our politics covered the spectrum, yet we established a strong sense of friendship and unity over those years.

Fairness

What is fair? The Random House College Dictionary gives this definition of fair, the adverb: "characterized by impartiality, unprejudiced."

I am continuously shocked at how revolutionary the concept of fairness can be. In order to be genuinely fair, the ideas must be fair to everyone across the spectrum of beliefs and ideals. Too often we are more concerned to what is fair to our own perspectives than to what is fair and inclusive to all perspectives. It is common, in the cultural wars, that when we think of fairness we are actually considering who is to blame. Genuine fairness is a process of navigating through multiple opinions to a discovery of greater good and does not look backward to blame but positively looks for the best way forward. How do we get out from under the tyranny of our own opinions and see clearly the thoughts, needs and perspectives of others? It could begin with the simple question, "Is it fair?" There is nothing magical in the question. There must be some heartfelt need for respect and fairness for everyone, not just ourselves. If sincere emotional content does not back up our search for fairness, then this is just one more piece of rhetoric subject to misuse and abuse. But if we deeply desire an end to isolation, disconnection and feeling like misfits in our own world, then fairness and respect could be a powerful starting point for change.

A Matter of Respect

As our curiosity allows us to gather information from others, we must determine how we will respond. If our primary objective is to convince others of the truth of our own perspective then we are unlikely to continue in any kind of healing conversation. What if we accepted that our primary responsibility in a healing conversation is to show the deepest respect for others.

Respect is vital. My definition of respect is *the heartfelt belief that every person I meet, from every walk of life, from every belief system, from every political perspective, from every race, culture, background and world view has something important to teach me.* I realize this is a hard concept and that we've all had experiences with negative people. While some people will fall outside the lines of this concept, it is a worthy attitude with which to approach life and relationships. (Review the chapter on trust when needed!)

Respect for Diversity

Jesus taught that there was power and true functionality in diversity. For years we have understood that the secret to the success of a nation or a corporation or a church or a family is in its ability to use diversity to grow stronger, deeper and wiser instead of seeing diversity as a threat. Somewhere along the way we have inadvertently begun to believe that the goal is to be homogenous. That would mean we must find some intellectual, social, emotional, spiritual or cultural plane on which we are all the same. Often in our culture it seems huge amounts of energy go into seeking this fictitious place where everyone becomes the same.

We seek political platforms where we can all agree. We seek social change which everyone supports. We seek environmental policies where the solution is obvious to everyone. The trouble is, that is not only impossible, it is also not using our strengths. The ideal is that we sit down with very different people and listen and show respect for the very diverse perspectives that emerge from real conversation. When we have heard and understood, we don't do battle to change the perspective of others, we do battle to find solutions that address very real needs and issues.

Our tendency to gather together with people who think, act and talk just like we do often blinds us to very important issues we are missing. The urge to seek safety drives us to listen to people that affirm us instead of challenge us. Our need for affirmation drives us to seek our own kind. It is very difficult these days to confront and disagree agreeably. Conflict is most often couched in our society as a winner-take-all kind of event.

Respect demands that we move away from such practices. Respect demands that conservatives believe that liberals have something of great value to share and teach. Respect demands that liberals believe the same about conservatives. Men believe that women are to be respected: their persons, their views, their feelings. Women believe men deserve the same respect. Christians believe it about Muslims, or Hindus, or agnostics and atheists. Muslims believe it and Hindus and every other world religion. Ethnic groups believe it about each other. Democrats believe it about Republicans and vice versa.

This demand for respect means we can no longer support leaders who do not show respect for the diversity of our world. Any leader that has not learned the fundamental lesson of respecting others is not qualified to lead. They are lost in their subjectivity and such subjectivity leads to blindness. Blindness leads to poor decision making. How can a leader be a leader if he or she consistently makes poor decisions? That is the very heart of leadership. In fact, what is leadership if not pulling together people of diverse perspectives and opinions for the greater good?

Tolerance Versus Respect

There is a lot of talk today about tolerance. We are admonished in our culture to be tolerant of others. That sounds incredibly passive and very generic. Tolerance, as a concept, has the common connotation of allowing something to exist. So, regarding others, many take that to mean that they should be willing to let others exist. I have heard this said many times: "I will tolerate them. I can tolerate them by not saying anything bad about them, ignoring them, overlooking them, or simply pretending they don't exist." When pressed, people admit, "Tolerance does not demand much from me. It certainly doesn't demand that I engage with people who are radically different than me. It does not demand that I share relationships with the other people on my planet. I just have to tolerate them."

Respect demands much more than tolerance. Human beings are designed to be relational. We are designed to connect with other human beings and, as a result of these connections, to grow in our understanding, wisdom, and perspectives. It's old and trite, but it is also profoundly true, we really do need each other. In all our diversity, politics and opinions, we deeply need each other.

Sharing Respect

This issue of showing respect doesn't begin with a revolution. It begins when people like you and me begin to show regard and esteem in the relationships we already share. Do you show respect for the people with whom you are sharing this journey? Let's start right within the immediate circle of the family. How many husbands genuinely respect their wives? I'm not asking how many *say* they respect their wives. How many husbands believe and then act upon the belief that their wives have insights, understanding and abilities that could bring desperately needed strengths to their home and marriage? How many wives believe that about their husbands?

In my experience as a minister (and granted usually it's the couples that are in the greatest pain that come to see me) many couples are trying to convince their partners to see things their way. They are seeking to be homogenous. There is a significant difference between being compatible and being complementary. So many relationships could be transformed by making that simple shift. We are not the same, but we are both better because of our diversity. I am a strong believer that we have some instinctive sense that draws us towards people who possess strengths and abilities that we lack. The old saying "opposites attract" is hinting at this instinctive reality. Sadly, what tends to attract us in the beginning tends to annoy us later on! Why? Because we don't continually create ways to make those differences be exciting and strengthening.

Do you show that kind of respect for your children? They are unique human beings with strengths, weaknesses, hopes, hurts and fears. They also have hearts, minds and spirits that offer the family something of great value. Each child brings something important to the life of the family. Can you name what that is in each of your children, or nieces and nephews, or grandchildren? Too often we spend time and energy trying to get our children to conform to an ideal. Certainly discipline, accountability and responsibility are important to instill in our children, but those lessons are much more easily taught to a child that feels esteemed, honored and respected than to a child that feels invisible and insignificant. Some of the most deadening things to the human spirit are when a person shows disapproval, disappointment, and displeasure.

The generation gap is the disconnection that occurs when generations forget that respect is due to each generation. When we become prejudiced about Boomers, Millennials, Gen-xers, or Gen-yers we are undermining the basic premise of respect. Each generation has something to teach. If we fail to listen and learn, we do so at our own peril. We, as a society, are losing. We are unable to evolve effectively and still hang on to values that matter. We tend to throw one over in favor of the other, but we are better together. We really do need each other's viewpoints and perspectives. It keeps the machinery of culture moving.

Is that true of you in the workplace? Do you nurture diversity and believe that the people with whom you work, each one of them, has something to teach you? Is that true for you personally in the political realm? Do you believe that people who do not share your political views are vital to a healthy culture, world, country and government? Is it true in your friendships or do you only befriend people who already think and act like you? Respect is not a theory. It is a commitment to a belief. It is the heartfelt belief that every person I meet, from every walk of life, from every belief system, from every political perspective, from every race, culture, background, and world view has something important to teach me. The belief leads to active, practical application.

When was the last time you showed an attitude of respect to those closest to you? When have you modeled respect on issues of politics, religion, social justice and the environment? Do you have the habit of showing disapproval, displeasure, disappointment and disrespect to others; even by raising an eyebrow or rolling your eyes? It's time to model respect. This takes discipline and a commitment to emerge from our subjectivity and practice what is simply fair.

Noah

Of all the Biblical stories that seem to get people going, the one of Noah is a frequent topic. From time to time I will engage in a "God Questions" series and Noah always makes the top five of people's questions. People want to know if I believe two of every animal made it onto the ark. They often want to understand why the God of the story wiped out everyone. I don't pretend to have all the answers, but one application of the story does stand out to me. If you step back from the narrative just a bit, then this story involves a family. The world in which the family lived was full of people of diversity. Different cultures, beliefs and temperaments. There's a ton of conflict and general meanness going on.

As the narrative unfolds, every person on the planet is removed from the conflict save this one family—just one family, one ethnicity, one language, one culture, one seat of beliefs, one set of values. Given this highly homogenous world, how long was it before conflict, anger, and hatred got reintroduced into the world? They didn't even make it one generation. Noah's sons end up in tremendous conflict.

Maybe the message is that getting rid of those who disagree with us is not the answer! Maybe the problem is less about the people in the world who do not share our beliefs and much more about something within us. Respect means that I am committing to see the world differently. I am committing to see people as having great worth. I am committing to seeing the people with whom I am sharing this journey and with whom I desire healing conversation with a newfound, and deeply seated kind of respect! Last I checked all were created in the image of God!

Chapter 13

Middle Ground

The "golden mean" is the middle road which guides
us through the extremes of life

Seeking

A few years ago, I was working with a couple in a struggling marriage and we had been at it for a while. There was a growing frustration in each partner. They both felt that their needs were quite simple and easily met if only their spouse would pay attention. At some point the exasperated husband said, "All I really want her to do is make me a bologna sandwich and be nice to me! Is that too much to ask?"

There is a sense in which we all feel that our needs are very simple. We want to be understood and cared for. That could be as simple as a nice smile and a sandwich. When was the last time you turned to your spouse and gave him or her a dazzling smile;

full of promise, playfulness and love? Not everyone can distill their needs down to such a point of simplicity. We are really seeking to have a deep need in our souls cared for. Now, we need a method that allows our deepest and most diverse needs to be met. Interestingly, the ancients understood this need and explored it completely.

The Golden Mean

Aristotle lived from 384 BCE to 322 BCE. He was a student of Plato and became the private tutor of the young son of Philip of Macedon, Alexander. Alexander would one day conquer much of the known world and be remembered as Alexander the Great. At some point Alexander wept because there was no more world to conquer! Through Alexander, Aristotle's thoughts were spread across the world. Aristotle began with his own questions about life: "What is the best life?" "What is virtue?" "What is life's supreme good?" "How do we find happiness and fulfillment?" Like the Hindus before him, Aristotle concluded that we all want to be happy.

Even the pursuit of goodness is rooted in the fact that we believe goodness leads to happiness. Of course, being a philosopher, Aristotle believed that we could reason our way to happiness. The ultimate evolution of human thought would lead us to understand the content of happiness. Aristotle said, "Virtue and excellence depend on clear judgment, self-control, symmetry of desire, and artistry of means; this is the achievement of experience only in the fully developed man."

That's a highly intellectual way of saying that in fully developed human beings we need common sense, the ability to control ourselves, the awareness to recognize that we share common needs and that we participate in the intentional and well-learned skills and artistry needed to effectively move ourselves and our culture forward. It would be no stretch to think that Aristotle believed that the "artistry of means" was the art of real, genuine and healing conversation. The content of that conversation is vital and Aristotle described it by proposing that "The road to this happiness is the Golden Mean."

Aristotle has provided us with a method that allows our deepest and most diverse needs to be met and it is the goal of truly healing conversations.

Listen carefully: The Golden Mean is the middle road which guides us through the extremes of life. So that would mean that the content of our conversation is not seeking to convince others of our perspective, but collectively seeking a middle ground between extremes. For Aristotle that meant that between cowardice and rashness is courage; between stinginess and extravagance is generosity; between sloth and greed is ambition; between secrecy and talking too much is honesty; between depression and buffoonery is good humor and so on. On one side of most issues there is excess and on the other there is deficit.

In summary, "truth", according to Aristotle, lies in the middle, in the Golden Mean. I contend that the real content of healing conversations should include seeking the middle ground between extremes. I've come to realize that the best way to know and to be known is to stop trying to convince others of our own perspectives and instead seek together the middle ground between us.

Blessed Are the Meek

Aristotle may not rock your world, but he's not the only person who advocates for the beauty of the middle ground. Matthew; chapters 5-7 contain what has come to be known as the Sermon on the Mount. In these teachings Jesus opens with one of the most famous of all His teachings, the Beatitudes with these words, "Blessed are…" If you break into the deeper meanings of the Greek in these passages, you learn some interesting things. First the phrases translated as, "Blessed are…" could more literally be translated as, "Participating in the joy of the gods are those who…" Jesus was teaching that these phrases are the key to having life and having it to the full.

These phrases are the key to knowing and being known. Each phrase has important values to teach, but let's focus on one of the most famous of them.

Matthew 5:5, "Blessed are the meek, for they will inherit the earth."

Jesus spoke these words in Aramaic which is an ancient and almost lost dialect of Hebrew. It was Matthew's task to translate those words into Greek. The word Matthew uses to best describe what Jesus is teaching in Matthew 5:5 is then translated into English as "meek." Meek doesn't have a lot of meaning for most of us and what meaning it does have is largely negative.

The word Matthew uses in the Greek, however, has huge implications for our everyday lives. Matthew uses the word "praus." Interestingly, this word is the same word used by Aristotle to describe the Golden Mean between extremes. Jesus, Himself, is teaching about the power of the middle ground in our very emotional worlds. That the Bible includes such a powerful reference to the wisdom of this middle ground is not only astonishing, but not what most of us think of when we think of meekness. William Barclay retranslates this verse:

> **Matthew 5:5,** "Blessed is the person who is always angry at the right time and never angry at the wrong time."

Middle Ground

How many of us consistently succeed at that? If we are to truly experience the power of healing conversations it will be rooted in a heartfelt belief that truth is found in the middle. I don't want to leave that point too quickly. We have adopted a mentality in our modern culture that the winner takes all. Politics has become a place where each party represents half the country. However, the ideal in our nation is that those in power represent all the people. Leaders don't favor some and vilify others. Yet, politicians do exactly that and so do we. We believe that our perspective is right and the perspective of others is wrong. We seek to win, but what if we deeply believed something better? What if we deeply believed that the truth is found in the middle? What if we came to believe that the truth was somewhere between what I believe and what "they" believe? What if we took seriously this staggering thought: "Participating in the joy of the gods are those who find the middle ground!"

Meekness points us to the middle. The Golden Mean calls our attention away from polarized thinking and solidly toward the middle ground. Healing conversations are balanced conversations between extremes. We may believe a lot of things, but we know very little. Our willingness to disclose our own beliefs and to practice curiosity about the beliefs of others begins to break open our abilities to hear and understand others. We respect the differences in others by believing that everyone has something important to teach us. That applies to perspectives and positions as much as it does to people. Over the top of all those important elements and perspectives we now add that the content of our conversations seeks a middle ground.

We have glamorized extreme positions in our culture. We have labeled people into distinct groups that are almost always polarized into caricatures. According to the ancients, the trouble with this way of thinking is that the truth seldom lies in the extremes.

I find the logic of that to be categorically true. The issues that confront our lives are very simple if we listen only to one side of the argument, but let a real conversation take place where the deeper underlying issues are revealed and suddenly you find yourself shifting your perspective. Suddenly, simple answers aren't as satisfying. More than once in my journey, I have cringed at the thought of what I did or said regarding a certain issue. I have read old sermons I have preached and found my words laced with ignorance. The ancients believed that it was a sign of a maturity to seek middle ground. For relationships to thrive, for our culture to thrive, we must stop seeing extremism as sound thinking. Extremism promotes ignorance. It excludes important information that is necessary for making informed decisions and for discerning truth. It may be entertaining to build and tear down paper tigers, but it serves no purpose in moving our lives forward.

Extremism has at least some roots in economics. Fund raising is made easier if one group distinguishes itself as the champion of right and then vilifies the opposing view. Creating frightening scenarios in which "our way of life" or "liberty" or "our values" are being threatened seems to inspire people to give to their respective causes. This way of marketing various points of view causes us to lose any sense of proportion. It leads us back to believing in a winner-take-all way of thinking.

Logically, we know that there is truth on both sides and a myriad of relevant and sometimes opposing issues to be considered, but emotionally we tend to go all in on one extreme perspective or the other. We must learn to be as emotionally and economically attached to the middle ground as we are to the extremes. That can only happen if we believe that what preserves our life, liberty and the pursuit of happiness, is truth and truth is most often found in the middle between the extremes.

Bringing It Home

Stop for a moment and think about the implications of a belief that truth lies in the middle ground between extremes. Apply that idea to your home and your family. Where does the deep conflict lie? Is it between you and your spouse? Is it between you and your oldest child? Is it between you and the in-laws? What would it mean for you to adopt a new perspective that says the truth is somewhere between how I see it and how my spouse sees it, or my child or my in-laws?

Most of us are fortified in our own beliefs, hurts and ways of thinking. We will not surrender what we think is the high ground. What would change if we confessed that we understand

and embrace that our views are only one side of the issue? In my experience, most spouses seem to find each other because of their differences. We are not alike. As I said before, I have come to believe that something instinctive in us is attracted to people who provide personality traits we lack. I don't necessarily think that opposites attract, but differences do. Instead of seeing ourselves in opposition to each other, what if we believed that our spouse represents some deep truth that if understood would make our marriage and life better? What if listening, and allowing the opposing view to move us toward the center, was actually the very definition of wisdom?

In healthy relationships the truth is in the middle ground between the extremes. Your child has a perspective and while parents must be parents, it is wise parenting to remember that the truth lies in the middle ground between extremes. It is true in our personal relationships and it is true in our society as well. What would happen to the respect between you and your child, or anyone else in your circle of influence, if you believed that not only do they have something to teach you but that the truth lies between you?

We as a culture seem to have a growing sense of dissatisfaction and anger. We are constantly waiting for the next election, or the next season, or the next legislation so the wrongs can be made right. We believe that the Democrats are ruining the country or Republicans are obstructionists. We distrust information unless it comes to us from the source that represents our own perceptions of reality. We espouse leaders who best articulate our perspectives. We choose talking heads who confirm what we already believe rather than challenge us to seek some redemptive truth in the middle.

Out of these passionate cries for one side to finally win out over the other, our society suffers. Where are the leaders who create consensus and show respect for people with an opposing perspective? Where are the courageous individuals who will no longer accept pejorative thinking and partisan politics? Where are the viewers and readers who will no longer tolerate bigotry from the "experts" who crowd the print media, television and radio waves? Where are the people who refuse to tolerate such things because those things reek of ignorance and simply do not work?

Where are the individuals who will no longer allow anyone in the family to be left out? Where are the homes that have decided that everyone, of every age, gender and ability, have something invaluable to share? Where are the individuals who see that the truth in our homes, families and friendships lies, beautifully, maturely and wisely between us and them? The truth most often lies in the middle ground between the extremes. Healing conversations seek this place of balance where we no longer defend our own opinions, but seek the golden mean and thus participate in the joy of the gods!

Chapter 14

Affirmation

We Enjoy Being in Conversations That Leave Us
Feeling Esteemed And Affirmed

The Easter Parade

A few years ago we were in the final planning stages for our Easter services. Every Sunday presents a seating challenge in our small buildings, but holidays reach the crisis level. Easter is annually celebrated in the huge local high school auditorium partly, for that reason. It's a full day. We value our families being able to worship together on such important days, and want to extend some special celebration that day to all our children. I thought it would be a great idea to have an Easter parade. Bring up the lights, invite our children forward, let everyone celebrate and appreciate their Easter best.

As the children moved forward, the crowd began to applaud. It was a natural response. The children soaked it up. They proudly marched forward and set themselves up across the front of the room. As they arrived they turned and faced the crowd. I expected the applause to die down. It didn't. It kept going and even started to build. I expected the children to be anxious to move on. They weren't. Instead they simply beamed while a room full of grown-ups offered them a thundering round of applause.

They showed no inclination to leave the warm glow of the moment and the crowd showed no interest in slowing the flow of affirmation and celebration. I'm not sure how long we just let that moment run on, but it was powerful. Even with the tight schedule and busy day, it was hard to let it end. The children finally had to be escorted out by the staff. I think they would have stayed all day. We take for granted our deep need for affirmation. I'm sure very few of the children could tell you why their instinct was to just stand still and smile and drink in this outpouring of encouragement, but you and I know. Our souls thirst for affirmation. Our hearts become sore and tired without it. Affirmation is vital to our sense of well-being and should grace all of our conversations and interactions.

Affirmation Defined

Paul gives us a powerful working definition of affirmation.
"Do not let any unwholesome talk come out of your
mouths, but only what is helpful for building others
up according to their needs, that it may benefit those
who listen." Saint Paul, Ephesians 4:29

This is a challenging piece of advice to apply to life and its nuances are very intricate. Paul is offering us a very well thought out and somewhat open definition of affirmation.

No Unwholesome Talk

Affirming words do not contain words that are unwholesome, but what does that mean? Unwholesome seems open to opinion. It's a word that might be defined in a variety of ways. Some days we might decide that unwholesome talk is anything negative or critical. On another day, it might mean words that are profane or rude. For some of us just petty and inappropriate words might be considered unwholesome.

Words That Build Up

Affirming words are also words that build up, according to Paul. If I am truly seeking to define words of affirmation, I have two hints from Paul's writing; they are to be wholesome and they are to build up, but both concepts are very subjective. Can't we define the idea a little more precisely? Of course. Paul has not finished his thought.

According to Their Needs

The words we choose to speak are to build up others according to their needs. That explains why Paul has kept the first two ideas a little vague. We are to speak no unwholesome words and build up based on the very specific needs of the person to whom we are speaking! These are not one-size-fits-all words. Affirming words speak very directly to the individual's needs and circumstances. Paul wants his readers to consider that truly life-giving words are custom-tailored to the person to whom they are spoken. If we haven't gotten the message yet, Paul takes it one step further.

It Must Benefit the Listener

Affirming words are to benefit the listener. Most of us have found ourselves arguing with someone who has taken offense at words we knew to be affirming. We are appalled that our affirming words are not appropriately appreciated. When I stop and realize that I have had such conversations, I feel silly for missing the obvious wisdom of Paul's guidance. Affirming words are not defined in my head and in my heart. The right to call words affirming does not belong to the speaker...it belongs to the listener...and that changes everything!

Affirmation

And so, the last element of a healing conversation is affirmation. When we discussed humility, I shared the words of 1 Corinthians 8:1b, "But knowledge puffs up while love builds up."

Humility addresses the issue of "knowledge puffing up." Affirmation invites us to allow "love to build up." If we are to enjoy and sustain healing conversations, we will need to pay very close attention to the art of affirmation. The goal of healing conversations is to build up. To walk through a conversation that is full of the vulnerability of trust, humility, self-revelation, curiosity, respect and middle ground requires something that also soothes the soul. That would be deep and meaningful affirmation.

I honestly believe that every single conversation and interaction in our lives would benefit from a commitment to affirmation. I suggest that conversations consisting of edifying talk suitable for building us up, is something we long for. I believe we all desire to receive such affirmation from others. We find it more difficult to offer the same to others, but affirming conversations requires intentionality and vigilance. Affirming words are wholesome and that wholesomeness is based on the culture, experience, age, background and beliefs of the person to whom we are speaking. This requires a special kind of sensitivity.

Again, affirming words build up according to the need of the listener. That requires that we pay attention to the circumstances of the lives around us. What builds up someone one day might not build up that person on another day. The emotional state of the person we are seeking to affirm will also impact our ability to build up. This need for fully integrated understanding and empathy is at the root of why we do not practice and enjoy more affirming conversations. All of this sensitivity is engaged with the sole purpose of building up and edifying those who listen.

Let's recognize for a moment that not all affirming words are necessarily words that are easy to hear. If we are going to be honest with others in a healing conversation, it seems important to acknowledge that not all the words can be sweet and soft. Healing conversations by their nature must sometimes be hard conversations. I am not advocating that healing conversations be superficial or laced with flattery, not at all! That said, affirmation is much, much more than the content of a conversation or the words chosen to express it. Affirmation is the ethos in which all healing conversations must take place.

Affirmation creates an atmosphere where every word spoken is intended for only one purpose "…to build up others according to their needs that it may benefit those who listen." Affirmation, encouragement and validation become the ultimate sanctuary in which healing conversations occur. As such, it is full of positive, loving intent. Words are used to weave together acceptance and celebration of the conversation so that those willing to risk themselves in such a way leave that space feeling built up. Few of us naturally offer even the most passing conversation with the gift and ethos of affirmation. That ethos must be nurtured and created by real words, real expressions, a lightness of heart, and purity of intent.

How often do you think of ending conversations with some words of affirmation? Do you think it's important? Do you feel valued when someone leaves you with genuine affirmation? Again, this is not about offering empty, glib flattery. It is about recognizing that people matter and that we want them to walk away from a conversation with a deep sense that something good has been accomplished. Practicing affirmation certainly helps build better relationships, but it also forces us to watch and listen with the intent to place an emphasis on the positive. That changes the very nature of our conversations. It sets the mood as warm, inviting and affirming. Such a place invites people to come back over and over and over. We enjoy being in conversations that leave us feeling esteemed and affirmed.

When we are committed to leave every conversation with a sense of affirmation, people will naturally seek that place of safety with us. They feel safe enough to hear hard things because these truths are spoken in love. In such a place, no unwholesome talk is used. What is used is only that which is suitable for the building up of others according to their needs, that it may benefit those who listen. Healing conversations must traffic in the content and ethos of affirmation. We want to leave people...better than we found them!

Chapter 15

Healing Conversations:
Truth, Beauty and Real Love

We Alone Have an Inexhaustible Voice

In 1950, William Faulkner won the Nobel Prize. He used his acceptance speech to speak into a world culture that was newly aware of the threat of nuclear destruction. In the years following the detonation of the first atomic bombs, the world lived in fear and worry at the possibility of the world literally blowing up, and this, for the first time in human history. This preoccupation with fear had become so prevalent that even the writers and artists had drifted in their focus from beauty and the truest conditions of the human heart, to thinking about world conflict, politics and social needs.

Faulkner used his speech to call those writers and artisans back to talking about what matters most. Here is a piece of that speech, edited a bit to have more inclusive language:

"Our tragedy today is a general and universal physical fear so long sustained by now that we can hardly bear it. There are no longer problems of the spirit. There is only the question: When will I be blown up? Because of this, the young man or woman writing today has forgotten the problems of the human heart in conflict with itself which alone can make good writing because only that is worth writing about, worth the agony and the sweat.

"(We) must learn them (the problems of the human heart) again. We must teach ourselves that the basest of all things is to be afraid...leaving no room in our workshops for the old verities and truths of the heart, the old universal truths without which any story is ephemeral and doomed. (We must include) love and honor and pity and pride and compassion and sacrifice. Until we do so, we labor under a curse. We write not of love but of lust, of defeats in which nobody wins anything of value, of victories without hope and, worst of all, without pity or compassion. Our griefs grieve on no universal bones, leaving no scars. We write not of the heart but of the glands.

"Until we relearn these things, we will write as though we stand and watch the end of humanity. I decline to accept the end of humanity. It is easy enough to say that humans are immortal simply because we will endure; that when the last ding-dong of doom has clanged and faded from the last worthless rock, hanging tide-less in the last red and dying evening, that even then there will still be one more sound: that of our puny inexhaustible voices, still talking.

"I refuse to accept this. I believe that humanity will not merely endure: we will prevail. We are immortal, not because we alone among creatures have an inexhaustible voice, but because we have a soul, a spirit capable of compassion and sacrifice and endurance. The poet's, the writer's, duty is to write about these things. It is their privilege to help humanity endure by lifting their hearts, by reminding them of the courage and honor and hope and pride and compassion and pity and sacrifice which have been the glory of our past. The poet's voice need not merely be the record of humanity, it can be one of the props, the pillars to help us endure and prevail."

Faulkner's words of calling humanity back from a focus on fear, lust, and the most common of human impulses are timely in our culture today for an entirely different set of reasons. The destructive nature that threatens us is not limited to super powers and weapons of mass destruction. The threats of today form their battle lines inside the hearts and minds of every human being. We are fighting a war of internal values and what is at risk is our regard for the worth and dignity of humanity. In the face of the nuclear threat, Faulkner called leaders to move the conversation toward the things that matter most, love, hope compassion and sacrifice. Our words have endless possibilities, because of the soul has God placed in us. That soul gives us, as Faulkner so powerfully observes, "an inexhaustible voice." It is a voice we should use wisely.

The Turning Point

Jesus was profoundly gifted at reminding us of the ways we are to use these inexhaustible voices. In Matthew's gospel, when He is asked by an expert in the law to offer up the greatest commandment, He offers up a response that should have surprised no one. He quotes from the creedal statement of Jewish tradition, The Shema. This prayer begins with a quotation from Deuteronomy 6:4, "Hear O Israel, the Lord is our God, the Lord is One." It includes the call to love the Lord our God with all of our heart, soul, mind and strength. The full response of Jesus goes further.

> **Matthew 22:34–40** (NIV). **34** Hearing that Jesus had silenced the Sadducees, the Pharisees got together. **35** One of them, an expert in the law, tested him with this question: **36** "Teacher, which is the greatest commandment in the Law?"
>
> **37** Jesus replied: "Love the Lord your God with all your heart and with all your soul and with all your mind." **38** This is the first and greatest commandment. **39** And the second is like it: "Love your neighbor as yourself. **40** All the Law and the Prophets hang on these two commandments."

We are invited by Jesus to use these inexhaustible voices to give honor to God and honor to others. We are to raise our voices to promote truth, beauty and real love.

The Seven Elements of a Healing Conversation

Through these pages I have tried to describe what I believe is a practical application of loving God and loving others. These thoughts are really observations I've made of people in crisis over the last thirty plus years. To truly love; to truly find our greater purpose; to truly experience the joy of loving and being loved, knowing and being known, we need to engage in the intimate art of expressing ourselves through the gift of healing conversations.

We must think with and practice the lost art of engaging, fulfilling and genuinely enjoyable conversations. The seven elements become a part of our personality. We don't stumble or fumble around with the steps of conversation; we dance the dance of conversation. We feel the rhythms within us. As we grow, we may discover that the dance has many more elements that bring about more life and joy. There is no limit to what we may learn, but we can begin with dancing these elements:

+ **Trust**
+ **Humility**
+ **Self-Disclosure**
+ **Curiosity**
+ **Respect**
+ **Balance**
+ **Affirmation**

It matters how we speak. It matters how we love. It matters what we believe about life and our own purposes in it. It matters what we decide to speak with our inexhaustible voices.

Truth, Beauty and Real Love

A few years ago I made the drive from the northern foothills of Los Angeles, down the 5, jumping on the 60, connecting to the 710 so I could run south right into the heart of Long Beach. The 710 dumps you right into the harbor. I made my way around to the south side of the harbor and parked in a designated spot in front of the Queen Mary. It's an amazing and grand old ship that is now a hotel and entertainment center. I was scheduled to perform a wedding in the chapel and pray at a reception in one of the grand ballrooms.

Stepping into the chapel is surreal. It's old world from a different time, a different era. You can feel the romance. I know it's probably silly, but I felt like I was joining a small fraternity of people who had been privileged to stand in that chapel, aboard that ship, and join two people in marriage.

I wondered how many weddings had happened at sea, outbound to Southampton, United Kingdom, or in-bound to New York. In that little room, now filled with people anticipating magical moments; hopes and dreams have been launched. Unlike a local church, this space must have hosted hundreds if not thousands of such ceremonies since the ship was launched in 1934. That's a huge number of hopes and a huge number of dreams. What do you think all those couples were hoping and dreaming?

I've been privileged to do many, many weddings. I am even more privileged to spend precious weeks talking to couples in preparation for their weddings. Those conversations always turn out to be more about their lives. And they always end with my encouraging them to dream big and affirming they can achieve big dreams.

I was at a wedding recently and the maid of honor offered a reading in her toast. I liked it so much; I went and looked it up. In his book, The Bridge across Forever, Richard Bach writes:

"A soul mate is someone who has locks that fit our keys, and keys to fit our locks. When we feel safe enough to open the locks, our truest selves step out and we can be completely and honestly who we are; we can be loved for who we are and not for who we're pretending to be. Each unveils the best part of the other. No matter what else goes wrong around us, with that one person we're safe in our own paradise. Our soul mate is someone who shares our deepest longings, our sense of direction. When we're two balloons, and together our direction is up, chances are we've found the right person. Our soul mate is the one who makes life come to life."

That seems to me to be the result of some very ambitious thinking about relationships. It represents a pretty high concept of love and marriage. Maybe, some would say, even unrealistic. C.S. Lewis argues in The Abolition of Man that the conditioners of our culture are seeking to breed cynics—that our young are being enslaved to a "cold vulgarity." He suggests that the job of every grown up is to help young people to recognize that the universe is such a place where truth, beauty, and love really exist.

I feel like that's a part of my job, to help young people realize that the universe is a place where truth, beauty and real love exist. I think it's the job of every grown-up. I think we should not only be helping the young people, but the wounded people, and the lonely people, and the discouraged people, the unsettled people, and the people full of longing. A great outcome of that help would be that people come to realize that truth, beauty and love exist within them!

It would be easy for the emphasis on romance to overwhelm us and cause us to forget that our love for each other is, finally and ultimately, the truth about us. The Bible suggests the the quality of the love we share reveals the depth of our connection to the divine. As we love God we are enabled to truly love each other. This love is not reserved only for the context of romance and marriage. On the contrary, we are invited to build relationships of truth, beauty and real love.

Gifts and Abilities

In 1 Corinthians 12, Paul is speaking about what it means to be a person of some particular talent. In our culture we seem to believe that the better, or more useful your talents and gifts, the more valuable you are in society. The better your talents and gifts, the more entitled you are to a happy life, great relationships, and the fundamentals: happiness, peace, joy, and contentment. It turns out all that talk about gifts and talents, was a set up. It turns out that life and happiness and being of immense worth has nothing to do with our talents and gifts. It has to do with something much more basic and something in which each of us is invited to participate.

He says it this way:

> **I Corinthians 13:1-8, 13** "And now I will show you the most excellent way. If I speak with the tongues of men and of angels, but have not love, I am only

a resounding gong or a clanging cymbal. If I have the gift of prophecy and can fathom all mysteries and all knowledge, and if I have a faith that can move mountains, but have not love, I am nothing. If I give all I possess to the poor and surrender my body to the flames, but have not love, I gain nothing. Love is patient, love is kind. It does not envy, it does not boast, it is not proud. It is not rude, it is not self-seeking, it is not easily angered, and it keeps no record of wrongs. Love does not delight in evil, but rejoices with the truth. It always protects, always trusts, always hopes, and always perseveres. Love never fails. But where there are prophecies, they will cease; where there are tongues, they will be stilled; where there is knowledge, it will pass away. And, now these three remain: faith, hope and love. But the greatest of these is love."

It is my prayer that healing conversations become one of the pathways that leads to the realization that the universe is a place where that kind of truth, beauty and real love exists. May each of us raise our inexhaustible voice while in the dance of healing conversations and speak of courage, honor, hope, pride, compassion, and sacrifice—the glory of our lives and the hope of our future.

Study Guide

The following is a guide for teachers, pastors and students of any age to put into practical use the principles outlined in this book. I've broken it down into chapters so that, as needed, you can review and reread. The questions can be used to help yourself, your relationships and your groups. Have fun with these, they should unearth lots of treasures amidst the dirt!

Chapter 1: It Is So Funny How We Don't Talk Anymore

Let's Talk

People seem lonely, in general, don't they? Please share your observations on this. As I go about my work as pastor, I encounter lonely people just about everywhere. At the grocery store the other day I was walking toward my car with a single bag of tomatoes. A complete stranger, an older woman, walking in the other direction, turned around and spoke up, "So, you chose the Roma tomatoes?"

"Uhhhh, yes, I did!"

Earlier, I had heard this lady chatting in line to a total stranger about her son and his work. In that moment, it occurred to me that she really wanted to talk. So, I took the time to talk with her about Roma tomatoes.

In reflecting, I realized she had a very small grocery bag—food for just one. I was buying the last forgotten items for a big family dinner—all the kids were coming to eat. I guessed she had prepared many such family meals in her past, but for tonight she was cooking for just herself. We talked, connecting at the level you can in a store parking lot. We both left smiling.

It's so funny how we don't really talk anymore. Is it a lost art that in the past offered guidance in a world of loneliness? Let's recover that lost art!

Just Curious

1. Do you recall a time when you were caught in a "Roma Tomato" conversation?
2. Are there people in your circle who frequently "need" to talk to you?
3. At a personal level, are you aware of the people around you when you are in public places? Their demeanor? Their circumstances? Their need for connection?
4. How about at social events or family events? Do

you notice people's individual dispositions? Do
you read their moods?

5. How do you generally assess the people you
    encounter? Threatening? Moody? Withdrawn?
    Invisible? Needy? Hostile? Lonely?

A Little Self-Disclosure

1. Do you recall your last deeply meaningful and
    connected conversation? Where? When? Who?
2. What made it so meaningful?
3. Are such conversations rare for you?
4. Were you the one driving that conversation or
    was someone else leading?
5. What percentage of your conversations is logis-
    tical? Agenda driven? Relational?
6. Do you feel you are good at meaningful conver-
    sation? Do you think those with whom you share
    relationship would agree?
7. How often do you feel that you are right and
    others should listen?
8. Are you intentional about creating "empty
    space" for people in conversation?
9. On a scale of 1-10, rate your own loneliness.
10. How do you relate feelings of loneliness to
    meaningful conversation?

Thank You, Thank You, Thank You!

Talking, even in a guided conversation like this one, is a
little risky. It's interesting that conversations are more mean-

ingful the more another person joins in. They get momentum when we are curious about the feelings and experiences of those around us and they become sacred when we choose to disclose how we really feel and what we truly think. Thank you for talking!

Chapter 2: Unsettled

Let's Talk

In one of the early treatments of this chapter, it was reviewed by a friend of a friend…you know some objective input. The overriding response from the reviewer was, "Is he ok?"

That's interesting to me. I really appreciated a total stranger reading these words and worrying about me, but it also confused me a bit. It seems that the admission that someone is unsettled creates unease in us. I can't speak for others, but I long for the world to be ok and I know that the lady worrying about me does, too. I long for people to be ok, to find happiness, contentment and fulfillment. So, I can understand why finding people unsettled can be…unsettling!

There's a pressure to be well-adjusted, mature, on point, have it together and generally be successful. I think it's a big deal. However, I think life defies being all settled. I think it's ok to be unsettled. The longer I live and the longer I serve in ministry, the more I deeply value people who are unsettled enough to always keep searching, asking, seeking and knocking. For the record I am unsettled and I'm ok.

Just Curious

1. How many people in your current relationships seem to be settled?
2. What indicators do you have that they are settled?
3. What indicators might suggest they are unsettled?
4. How often do you talk about the unsettledness in these relationships?
5. What topics usually reveal the unsettledness in others?

A Little Self-Disclosure

1. How does being around unsettled people make you feel?
2. Do you prefer to talk to people who seem to be perfectly content or who are struggling?
3. How much do you associate being mature with being settled?
4. If you had to choose one area of life, what specific area makes you feel most unsettled?
5. If life could be neatly divided up into sections, would you say more of your "life" sections are settled or unsettled?
6. Do you see being unsettled as a strength or weakness? In what ways is it a weakness in your mind? In what ways is it a strength?
7. How important is it to you to be able to talk about the unsettledness in your own life?

8. Do you think that most people share the common experience of unsettledness?
9. Do you think that is talked about in constructive and consistent ways in your relationships?
10. How much do you think the people with whom you share relationship want to talk to you about their unsettledness?

Thank You, Thank You, Thank You!

It's so much easier to share things about which we feel confident and so much harder to share places where we are vulnerable and unsettled. Remember, that discussions of any kind thrive when people share honestly without dominating. So, take a minute to congratulate yourself for being willing to share. Take a moment to feel good about searching your own life honestly and practicing authentic feelings instead of "oughts." Now, take a minute to share with anyone in the group whose participation and vulnerability helped you. Thank you for thinking, talking and sharing!

Chapter 3: Longing

Let's Talk

When Jesus was asked, "What is the greatest commandment in the law?" He replied, "To love the Lord, your God with your whole heart and, to love your neighbor as yourself." Those simple thoughts give me much to think about. Specifically, I think the crowd to which Jesus spoke must have been more well-adjusted than most of us. They were simply to love their neighbors as *themselves*. Jesus assumed they loved themselves. There's a longing in us to love and be loved; to be loved by others, certainly, but to simply love ourselves? For many of us that would be a huge step forward.

The culture seems to steal away self-confidence, not build it. The culture tends to make room for those who fit nicely into categories even though the categories seem to be getting more and more polarized which means fewer and fewer of us fit comfortably. I long for a kinder and gentler world and not just in the overall, broad sense. In our personal worlds, most families, friendships and working relationships would better thrive with less extremism and a whole lot more turning together.

Just Curious

1. What distresses you most in the current cultural climate?
2. Are there specific extreme perspectives that worry you? Like what?
3. Do you have friends or family where certain subjects are off limits? If so, what are they?
4. Do you ever feel put down for your opinions on certain topics?
5. Do you feel friendships are getting easier or more difficult to maintain? Why?

A Little Self-Disclosure

1. Where do you turn for reliable information and facts regarding what's going on in the world?

What makes that source reliably truthful and fact based?

2. Do you mostly listen to people with whom you already agree or do you listen to people who challenge you? What feelings are associated with both experiences?

3. Do you find it is easy to have conversations about politics? Why? Or, why not?

4. Do you feel religion is helpful in sorting out truth? Can you easily talk about religion? Who with and who wouldn't you talk about it with?

5. Do you feel that education is still an impartial pursuit of truth? When is it or when isn't it?

6. How important is it for a society to be able to openly and freely discuss the ideals of human conduct?

7. How many meaningful conversations are you able to have about these overarching issues?

8. What kind of longing exists in you in regard to these issues?

9. How do you conduct yourself in such conversations? Aggressive? Dominating? Withdrawn? Passive? Conciliatory? Curious? Respectful?

10. Do you feel that anyone really knows the real you and likes you as you are?

Thank You, Thank You, Thank You!

There's longing in most of us to see things come together. We long to know and be known. The only way for such longings to be met are to talk about how we see the world, what fears we carry around, and what heartfelt beliefs drive us. Risking conversation about world views, politics and religion takes courage. If this conversation has gone well, whether from your perspective or that of the group, congratulations! I pray it's the first of many more. We are given the gift of communication and we are to use it to build up and not to tear down. Share with the group the refreshing things you saw and heard as people risked sharing. Thank you for engaging!

Chapter 4: Longing to Find a Tribe

Let's Talk

It's been said that there is strength in numbers. I grew up with a strong sense of belonging. I belonged in my family. I belonged in my church community. I belonged in my larger community. I felt connected and I felt I shared a lot in common with all those different people. So, in my growing-up years there were many communities into which I fit comfortably.

There are fewer groups where I feel genuinely at home, the older I get! There are very few places where I fit comfortably. As I've gotten older, I've learned to adapt and compromise to some extent. Politically, I don't fit into any one group so I find middle ground and choose viewpoints that I can own with integrity. But group wise, there is no group where I feel entirely comfortable, except those groups I create with and for other seekers. My questions about religion and faith can cause trouble instead of growth, so I choose a belief system where I feel a sense of integrity and truth. But I've noticed that many people I know pick a belief system that seems tolerable and they make do. There may be strength in numbers, but choosing a tribe can easily stunt our growth.

Just Curious

What tribes can you name that are prominent in the culture?

1. Are there people in certain tribes with whom you find it difficult to connect?
2. Do you think that's more about the tribe or the person?
3. What is good about finding a strong community that shares your beliefs?
4. What are some possible dangers about such a community?

A Little Self-Disclosure

1. How many tribes can you name in which you might have taken part at one time or another? (Politics, sports, religion, clubs, social networks.)
2. How much do you or did you identify with those tribes?
3. In what ways does the tribe make you feel secure?
4. In what ways do you feel the tribe misrepresents your own personal feelings?
5. Do you feel defensive of your tribe?
6. Do you find yourself feeling angry or adversarial to other tribes?

7. What traits do you find offensive in other tribes?
8. Do your attitudes reflect any of those traits?
9. Do you seek to understand the individuals with other tribes or do you tend to lump everyone together?
10. Do you find a sense of security from the tribal nature of our culture or do you experience more loneliness and longing?

Thank You, Thank You, Thank You!

Tribes are a convenient way to find belonging, but they can also cause divisiveness in our culture. Affirm those in the group who rise above their tribal identity and speak up for their own beliefs. Celebrate those who may be letting go of some group prejudices and are beginning to seek, listen and grow.

Chapter 5: Hiding in Our Chosen Type

Let's Talk

This chapter evolved from the story of Molly. It was a story she had shared with me about how she chose a persona to substitute for her true, authentic self when she was a teenager. This persona, a kind of mask or façade that satisfied the demands of her group, did not represent her inner personality. This persona ultimately harmed her.

At first, I didn't particularly think her persona choosing was necessarily universal, however, the more I thought about it the more I could see how I, too, had chosen "personas" in my life that were useful in forwarding some purpose, but which hid from view my true inner self.

Types, categories of people having common characteristics, can also be useful to navigate this world, but are often used to hide behind. I mean that people in types may or may not use personas behind which to hide and in so doing misrepresent themselves.

Identities are different from either personas or types and are very useful to adopt for letting others know what your job, gift or talent is and what to expect. Identities include: business person, accountant, doctor, lawyer, actor, director, producer, artist, housewife or househusband, rock star, pastor, athlete, etc.

While these three are different, there is overlap. Can you see that there are many "personas" "types" and "identities" there to choose from? I'm not sure we always knowingly choose types or if some are hardwired into us, but along the way it seems to me to matter less and less how we got our types and more and more how those types interfered with our ability to be wholly ourselves.

On the other hand, I find comfort in my chosen identity. It guides me in what to do, say and how to respond. I also recognize that my identity can limit me. Sometimes choosing an identity is a very positive choice of maturity, but sometimes, just like choosing a persona or adopting a type it can be a method of hiding in plain sight.

Just Curious

1. Define identity, type and persona. How are they different and how are they similar?

2. Name all the "types" that come easily to mind.
3. What are the "types" with whom you work?
4. What are the "types" with whom you go to church, to school and other groups?
5. How do "types" help you manage relationships?
6. How do they create disconnection?

A Little Self-Disclosure

1. Do you have a "type"?
2. Would your family say you have a "type"? Would your opinions be more likely to cause agreement or disagreement?
3. Are there certain "types" of people you avoid?
4. In what ways does or did a "persona" or "type" allow you to be yourself?
5. In what ways might your "type" prevent you from being fully yourself?
6. Do you regularly examine your life?
7. Do you believe you are objective in this?
8. Do you ever involve others in the process of self-examination?
9. How does choosing a "type" create stereotypical personalities?

Thank You, Thank You, Thank You!

It's a good time to be reminded that discussions are meaningful only to the level of participation they involve. Nowhere is it so quickly obvious than in a small group that great discussions involve people who are vulnerable and who fully engage.

Conversation is a place that thrives with meaningful input and suffers irreparably from distractions or lack of connection. Give a word of encouragement to those in the group who have risked and shared and been fully engaged.

Chapter 6: Relational Intimacy—The Missing Piece

Let's Talk

When couples come to me to perform their wedding ceremonies, I require six weeks of premarital counseling. One of the core principles of that counseling program shows that relationships are very seldom intuitive. We don't learn how to be great at relationships because we have some deep instinctive understanding of what works and what doesn't. Shockingly, that is the basic expectation of most couples I meet. It could be assumed that since attraction was instinctual, "how" to be in relationship should follow as easily.

We try to teach some things that can certainly be learned, but the learning can be painful. So, we teach a few things designed to help couples have a strong foundation on which to learn and grow. Relationships are not automatic. Great ones learn and grow and refine the art of healing conversations. I try to instill in young couples the concept that the dream for a great marriage is not a fairy tale, but the dream requires the two people who want it should be willing to invest time to listen, time to share, and time to mutually grow.

Just Curious

1. On a scale of 1-10 how would you rate the overall health of relationships among the people you know?
2. What things contribute to healthy, thriving relationships?
3. What things are key issues in relationships that struggle?
4. How much help do you think most people get in navigating their relationships?
5. From where does that help most often come?

A Little Self-Disclosure

1. How prepared were you for the relationships of adulthood? Friendships? Work relationships? Marriage? Children?
2. Who or what did the most to prepare you?
3. Where do you get the best guidance now when relationships struggle?
4. What attributes are most valuable to you in relationships?
5. What tools do you use to manage conflict?
6. Do you find conflict usually has a positive outcome?
7. Do past conflicts tend to build up?
8. Do you feel more cynical or optimistic about relationships in general?
9. Are there specific things that inspire those feelings?

10. Do you feel you are more of a veteran at relationships or more a novice who is still learning?

Thank You, Thank You, Thank You!

The topic of the quality and nature of our relationships is addressed in a very vulnerable space. The discussion above probably made for some discomfort and required some diplomacy. This is a good place to be reminded that attitude matters greatly when starting to talk about relational expectations, disappointments and hopes.

Words of encouragement help to create a sense of safety and hope for building bridges and opening up new possibilities. Criticism, hurt feelings, and anger close down meaningful conversation. Take a few minutes to affirm that the conversations that have a good outcome are about building deeper, better, more fulfilling relationships. We are all learning and often cannot grow unless we are taught.

Chapter 7: Words

Let's Talk

I am staggered by Frederick Buechner's thoughts in the quote from this chapter. To imagine that all of our poetry, history, wisdom and holiness are confined to the rearranging of the 26 letters of our alphabet is both overwhelming and strangely hopeful. Words are powerful tools. History tells us that they have infinite power to change the course of human life and of the course of the human narrative. If they can reframe the past and shape the future, then they can certainly have a profound impact on relationships.

The topic changes a bit here. No longer are we talking about how we got into the lack of communication. Now, we are starting to consider what we most believe about relationships. Words are powerful. Non-verbal communication is powerful. Being engaged is a message. Being disconnected speaks volumes. Do you believe that your words and the way they are delivered have the power to either create deep bonds or to sever emotional connection? This discussion is about deciding just how powerful you believe words to be.

Just Curious

1. In what ways do you see words used in detrimental ways in our society?
2. How do you feel about the choice of words among our leaders? Politics? Celebrities? Writers? Analysts? Teachers? Religious Leaders?
3. What are your pet peeves about the use of language within your relationships?
4. When was the last time you were deeply moved by someone's words?
5. Is there someone with whom you always enjoy sharing conversations? Why?

A Little Self-Disclosure

1. How careful are you of the words that you speak?
2. How much attention do you pay to the non-verbal

elements of communication? Eye Contact? Body Language? Facial expression? Tone?

3. Do you find yourself defending your use of words, attentiveness or tone?

4. Do you listen when someone challenges you on your communication skills?

5. Are you defensive about your intentions or attentive to what others hear?

6. How sensitive are you to the words of others, and, also, to non-verbal communication?

7. Do you believe that words are the primary way we weave together meaningful relationships?

8. What other ways are relationships created and developed? What other ways bring about growth?

9. Respond to these sentences from the chapter:

.   "Every human longing and emotion are addressed and healed, or shattered, by these letters thrown together and delivered nicely wrapped or carelessly thrown. They are received as unexpected gifts or as shrapnel posing deadly danger. It all depends on how they are arranged and how they are delivered."

10. What commitments do you feel are important for you to make in regard to your words?

Thank You, Thank You, Thank You!

Committing to watch our words and to acknowledge the power of words is fundamental to building deep and meaningful relationships. Would you take a minute to express your own hopes for using words to build up and not tear down? Share with someone what you appreciate about their use of words in this very vulnerable space.

Chapter 8: Trust

Let's Talk

Of all the things that I find difficult in being the father of four girls, the most heartbreaking is seeing them mistreated and having their trust broken. Now I'm sure that they've had their own moments of mistreating and breaking trust with others, but that's outside my experience. Over the years, it has become more and more clear that trust is a very precious building block of meaningful relationships. It is a vital element in deep conversation.

Trust is not a once and for all. We don't simply have it or lose it or lack it. We create trust daily. We practice faithfully all the elements that go into offering complete safety to another person or we neglect those elements at our peril and the peril of the relationship. This chapter is deeply personal and is focused on the underlying principle that each of us needs to be and provide a safe place for others. It also involves letting people into our castles who are committed to keeping us safe. The focus is not to keep people out, but to let the right people in.

These ideas of defensive lines in the approach to the castle are, of course, a metaphor, but I think they offer us ways of assessing our relationships. Of making informed decisions of what's going right and why some relationships hurt us. They also offer the hope of moving all our relationships forward or holding them sacred at a lesser place of vulnerability for now. Step one for healing conversations is developing trust.

Just Curious

1. Would you say trust is increasing in our culture or decreasing? Why?
2. How do you define trust and how important do you believe trust to be in relationships?
3. Is trust earned or given?
4. Do you believe people are entitled to trust because they are in relationship?
5. Is trust an all-or-nothing proposition? Why?

A Little Self-Disclosure

1. Can you think of a friendship where you shared the full run of the castle? What did that look like? How did that feel?
2. How common are such friendships for you?
3. Were they more common when you were younger? Why do you think that is?
4. What elements at the moat stand out to you? Do you do what you say? Are you reliable? Are you consistent?
5. What elements at the curtain wall stand out to you? Are you safe? Do you want to know about me? Are you preoccupied?
6. How are you at practicing true hospitality?
7. What elements at the drawbridge stand out? Is there mutual vulnerability? Is there willingness

to risk? Is there a willingness to meet needs and desires?

8. What elements at the grand gate get your attention? Are you committed to this relationship? What kind of relationship are you willing to create? Are you willing to keep investing in the relationship?

9. Do you believe you do all these things well? Would those with whom you share relationships agree?

10. How important is it to keep investing in the process of building trust?

Thank You, Thank You, Thank You!

Trust is not just about the relationships we share outside of moments of discussion and interaction. Trust profoundly affects the quality of learning together. Take a minute to express your appreciation for those in the group that make you feel safe and are creating a growing sense of trust for you. Go around the circle and share one thought in this session that you have committed to work on in your own relationships. Thank those who have shared in this vulnerable space.

Chapter 9: Humility

Let's Talk

I make it a frequent practice to say to my staff, "When you know what you are doing, you are a danger to yourself and others." I think that's incredibly true in ministry, but I'm not sure it is any less true in every other area of life. When we take what we believe and turn it into an unmovable foundation stone, we have a tendency to stop growing. Many tribal cultures did not believe that the deepest beliefs of the society should ever be written down. They were to be passed on by oral traditions, like storytelling, dance and the celebration of rituals. They distrusted the written form because it locked the truths into time and space. The oral tradition allowed for adaptation so the truth was always fresh and always relevant. Humility invites us to see our own beliefs and understandings as a fluid reality instead of fixed point. Knowing-best has a tendency to end all discussion. It also has a tendency to end all growth or even the sense that we need to grow. Relationships require humility in order for any real conversation to take place.

Just Curious

1. How would you rate the overall level of humility among leaders? Political? Work? Religion?
2. How does a lack of humility affect you personally?
3. What happens to you when you are around a person who lacks humility?
4. How do you react to the phrase, "I don't know much"?
5. In what way is truth absolute and in what way is it relative?

A Little Self-Disclosure

1. Do you consider yourself to be wise or unwise?

2. What process leads you to that understanding?
3. Do you often give advice?
4. Is that advice couched in humility or is it spoken as if absolute?
5. How much do you appreciate humility in others?
6. On a scale of 1-10 rate your own humility? Are you happy with that rating? Do you think those with whom you share relationships would agree?
7. How do you feel about Author, C.S. Lewis' definition of humility? "Humility is not thinking less of yourself, it's thinking of yourself less."
8. How often in communication do you fully tune into what another person is saying? What does this have to do with humility?
9. Do you have the courage to admit out loud that you really don't know much? Is that hard to do? What makes it difficult?
10. How deeply do you believe in the virtue of humility?

Thank You, Thank You, Thank You!

It is so important to practice humility. In a group setting, some feel the need to speak to every string of the conversation. Others sit back, listen a lot and make thoughtful contributions. Knowing when to speak and how much to speak is deeply rooted in humility. Share with others in the group your appreciation for those who seem to practice such humility. Share with the group your appreciation for those who admit the need to grow and are taking steps to embrace what they're learning.

Chapter 10: Self-Disclosure

Let's Talk

When the subject of Self-Disclosure comes up, I imme-diately realize that there is need for a disclaimer. As a pastor, it seems people who come to me for counseling feel almost compelled to self-disclose. Most of the time, it is a sacred experience. Sometimes it feels like mind-dumping and the words may spill far beyond the sacred. There is a difference between true healthy Self Disclosure and recklessly speaking every thought that comes into your head. If we are hidden, it is impossible for us to be known. If we disclose unwisely or endlessly, we will drive people away. Like all the forms of meaningful conversation, there is an art to the process of Self-Disclosure. It can only happen effectively where trust has been established. It happens much more easily with those who practice genuine humility. Self-Disclosure, if done right, is risky and vulnerable and I believe one of the most important gifts we can give to our relationships.

Just Curious

1. Do you recall a time when someone's Self-Disclo-sure spilled far beyond sacred space?
2. What emotions did you experience?
3. Can you recall a time when you stood on the sacred ground of Self-Disclosure as someone shared from their heart?
4. What emotions did you experience?

5. Are you generally closer to those who know all about you or to those who only know what you like them to know?

A Little Self-Disclosure

1. Do you like to talk about yourself?
2. Do you tend to keep things to yourself or talk too much or are you perfectly balanced?
3. Do you appreciate listening to people who tell their own vulnerable story?
4. Do you enjoy telling vulnerable stories about yourself?
5. Do you feel more comfortable giving advice or sharing your own struggles?
6. Are you more likely to lead with a story about yourself or just tell small pieces and wait to see if anyone wants to know more?
7. Self-Disclosure is a give and take. Do you consider yourself good at recognizing when someone is sharing and treating it as sacred ground?
8. How well do you listen and ask good clarifying questions?
9. How often do you feel someone treats your Self-Disclosure with an attitude of sacredness?
10. Do you ever consider that your own story is your greatest gift to your friends and family? Why? Why not?

Thank You, Thank You, Thank You!

Take a few minutes and think about the sacred space of Self-Disclosure. In closing this discussion, are there things that you would like to share that you've learned? Are there others in the group you would like to affirm for their willingness to be vulnerable and for the content of their self-disclosing that made you grow? In what ways could you make this space more inviting to those who are sharing?

Chapter 11: Curiosity

Let's Talk

I talk for a living, but I often feel I talk too much! And, I am really interested in trivial things! I store what I consider to be a lot of useless information in my brain and it's easy for me to see how the current topic of conversations relates to twelve pieces of trivia that I recall. Sometimes, mid-sentence, I feel I should just stop talking. I feel that especially when I share conversation with someone who is a good listener and is genuinely curious about me and my life. I don't want to take advantage of that gift and over share!

It amazes me how deeply I connect with someone who wants to know about me and my story. I've watched curiosity work in the counseling office. People leave transformed, encouraged, re-energized and what did they get from me? They got someone who just listened, offered empty space, didn't judge, leaned it, was curious about what was happening to them, wasn't pushing for an outcome, someone who just didn't talk too much. That is a rare space. We long for it and those around us long for it, too. Our family members long for it, our friends long for it, total strangers long for it. It may be the most sacred space on earth, a genuinely curious, listening heart, mind and spirit. It's a skill to be nurtured and improved.

Just Curious

1. Can you think of an individual in your life who is curious about you?
2. What do they do that makes you feel valued?
3. Can you recall a specific conversation that really re-energized you? What happened?
4. If you cannot think of such a conversation, why do you think such conversations are so rare?
5. How much do you think emotional connection has to do with individuals being genuinely curious about each other?

A Little Self-Disclosure

1. Do you talk too much? Would those with whom you are sharing relationship agree?
2. What emotions or thoughts run around in you when someone else is speaking to you?
3. Do you feel comfortable just listening?
4. What are the dangers for you in just listening?
5. What feelings trigger in you when someone genuinely expresses interest and curiosity about you?

6. What emotions trigger in you when someone is distracted, talks over you, or can't remember things you've shared?
7. Why do you think this is so damaging?
8. Do you believe that there is something genuinely healing and connecting about simply being curious about others? Explain.
9. What specific actions and words make you feel you are being listened to and valued?
10. What would you need to change in order to give those gifts to those with whom you are sharing relationship?

Thank You, Thank You, Thank You!

Take a minute to let this conversation sink in. Were things said that triggered some curiosity in you? Go back and speak to those who may have piqued your curiosity. A simple, "I'd love to hear more about that," would be a great way to extend the conversation past this moment. Express your appreciation for people in the group whose contribution helped you grow.

Chapter 12: Respect

Let's Talk

Fairness is almost a lost art. As our culture has become more combative, fairness has become a forgotten matter. There's not much fairness in the political realm. Politics stir up deep emotions, usually based in fear. We seem to tolerate unfairness from our own tribe, but become highly sensitive to it when it's used against us. Religions tend to be unfair. Dogma quickly replaces the heartfelt, loving Gospel of Jesus. We try to squeeze every human on the planet into a mold that we ourselves fit very poorly. It happens to us personally. If we are not careful, our thoughts and feelings become the "real" truth and everyone else is just being contrary. Once we've had our feelings trampled on a few times, it's easy for us to begin to label others.

We assign our own "types" to those around us. He's the disconnected type. She's the neurotic type. They are the high-maintenance type. She's elitist. He's just contrarian. Once we have those labels in place, we feel free to practice a sophisticated kind of disrespect. Boil it all down and our basic individual philosophies of life are far too often, "I am right and others are just wrong." That is a formula for deep divisions in the world, in a nation, in a church and in a family. It is still a very important part of relationships to practice fairness. Fairness is the by-product of an art and skill we should nurture; that of showing respect.

Just Curious

1. Take a minute to think over and share what you feel is unfair in the world.
2. Do a little analysis on the things that were shared.
3. What general categories came up?
4. How do you think fairness and respect are related?
5. What's the difference between tolerance and respect?

A Little Self-Disclosure

1. How do the areas of unfairness that you have shared impact you emotionally?
2. Why do you think that unfairness is an issue in the culture?
3. What damage does being unfair cause?
4. When you consider the issues that have been discussed, do you see ways in which you participate in the unfairness?
5. In what areas do you think you are unfair? In what areas do you think you are completely fair? Would those with whom you share relationship agree?
6. Do you feel respected by people who have a different perspective than you? Explain.
7. Do you think you fully respect people who have a different perspective from you? Explain.
8. Do you feel respected in your closest relationships?
9. Are you respectful in your closest relationships?
10. How important do you believe respect is in the process of healing conversations?

Thank You, Thank You, Thank You!

What words might need to be spoken at the end of this discussion to assure the people around you that you are seeking fairness? Can you share with the group steps you need to take in order to renew a sense of respect? Can you affirm those in the group who have spoken in ways that made you feel respected? Thank those in the group that are making this a rewarding experience for you.

Chapter 13: Balance

Let's Talk

For many years the idea of finding the middle way has been shaping my life. I love the philosophical and historical story of Aristotle. I love connecting his story to his predecessors and mentors, Socrates and Plato. I find his concepts about the golden mean to be enlightening and clarifying. When I realized that Matthew had borrowed Aristotle's word to translate the beatitudes about meekness it was an epiphany. It takes humility, respect, curiosity and sometimes just plain commitment to believe that the truth very often lies between me and those with whom I disagree.

I know that we can argue that the truth is never relative, but I am. My interpretation of the truth is almost always biased in my favor—even my spin on absolute truth. In forty years of ministry, I have learned some of my most profound truths from those outside the faith. It's an astonishing new way to think. I am a seeker of the middle ground. I am one who unites, not one who likes to divide. I can practice this simple principle of healing conversations with my child, my spouse, a stranger or anyone I meet. Seeking the middle ground is an honorable quest and it encourages truly healing conversations.

Just Curious

1. What percentage of people that you know would you characterize as polarizing?
2. What percentage of politicians do you consider polarizing?
3. Do you feel most issues are discussed in a way that encourages unity?
4. Do you believe in a "winner take all" philosophy in life?
5. Would you consider yourself to be a centrist[5] on most issues? The definition of "centrist" is: one that holds to well-reasoned views considerate of short and long-term needs

A Little Self-Disclosure

1. Do you more identify with one side of the political spectrum than the other?
2. Do you tend to see social issues more from one perspective than the other?

---

5   (politically) While there is no set rule for what a Centrist is, there are some generally accepted guidelines that seem to depict the Centrist mode of thought. Centrism is a political ideology based on reason and pragmatism considerate of short and long term thinking—Centrism is not defined by compromise or moderation, it is considerate of them. Centrism is about achieving common sense solutions that appropriately address current and future needs; support the public trust; and serve the common good with consideration of risk and capacity in context of these needs. Modern definitions sometimes conflate Centrism with moderation but the Centrist Party tenets generally oppose moderate views. Let's just call moderates 'moderates' and Centrists 'Centrist'.

Salient points about Centrism from the CP perspective: Centrism is not about doing what is popular, it is about doing what is right. Centrism is not moderate but rather supports strength, tradition, open mindedness and policy based on evidence not ideology. Centrism is not about compromise but rather allows for it as reasonable. http://uscentrist.org/about/party/what-is-centrist

3. Do you feel that your perspective is more right than the opposing perspective?

4. Do you feel your perspective must be limited given your background and experiences?

5. Why is it important that we admit that our perspectives are very limited?

6. Do you feel genuine respect for other perspectives? Why? Why not?

7. Do you believe that without diverse perspectives we can never arrive at the best solutions?

8. Are there diverse perspectives within your closest relationships?

9. Do they tend to be places of ongoing conflict?

10. In what ways would seeking the middle ground change the emotional climate of your world, both public and private?

Thank You, Thank You, Thank You!

Take a moment and reflect on the thoughts of this discussion. This is a life-shifting change. To begin to believe that we need the opposing voices if we are to ever arrive at the best solutions is a core principle of true diversity. The Bible suggests that we are one body and the diversity allows the highest functionality. History suggests that democracies are built of the principle of strength in diversity. Families function best in diversity. Marriages are rooted in diversity. How can you affirm to the group that truth is not something you know, but seek? How can you affirm that seeking the middle ground is an act of deep maturity and it inspires healing conversation? Take a moment to affirm those in the group that have helped you in this session or who have been most vulnerable.

Chapter 14: Affirmation

Let's Talk

If you were to ask any of the pool with whom I work how I could be better at my job, I think the number one answer would be, "To be more affirming." If you asked my family, I think their answer would be the same. We all need to be affirmed and to affirm others much more often. In our culture and in our relationships, there is a serious lack of acknowledgement for even the willingness to contribute as well as for actions and efforts that did contribute. We most often feel it when someone offers us some affirmation and we realize how much we've been longing for it and how long it has been since we've had much.

Words and affirmation are intimately connected. You cannot be affirming and fill the atmosphere with the pollution of negativity, criticism and pettiness. As we come to the close of these discussions, nothing is simpler to see or harder to change than the negligence of building up those around you. Affirmation is fuel for human joy, peace, and safety. The whole culture needs much more of this fuel in order to rekindle the fires of well-being. I'm guessing so does every home, family and relationship. As a friend of mine says, "admiration brings out the best in people."

Just Curious

1. How common is affirmation in today's culture?
2. How common is it in your place of work?
3. Is it common in your social network?
4. How common is it in your church, if you attend? How common do you think it should be and how should that be manifested?
5. How much do you think affirmation or negativity actually affect the atmosphere in which you live?

A Little Self-Disclosure

1. When was the last time someone spoke affirming words to you?
2. What was the setting?
3. Why did it matter so much?
4. If you can't recall a time, why do you think affirmation is so rare?
5. Is there someone in your life that consistently speaks words of affirmation? How do you connect to them emotionally?
6. How good are you at being affirming? Would those with whom you're sharing relationship agree?
7. Is it troubling to you that Paul suggests that the hearer gets to decide if it's affirming? Why?
8. What are the implications that the hearer decides for learning to be a person who practices the art of affirmation?

9. Would you be excited if the people in your circle of relationships committed to be more affirming to you? Why?

10. Are you excited to commit to be more affirming to the people in your circle of relationships? Why?

Thank You, Thank You, Thank You!

This would be the perfect time to speak words of affirmation to the people around you. Search your heart and offer genuine words of affirmation. Flattery and affirmation are not the same thing. One involves deeply thinking about why a person has had a positive impact on you and simply sharing that truth. Take your time and offer words that are genuinely affirming. Receive words of affirmation as well. Let them feed your soul. They are fuel for a deep sense of well-being. Commit to filling the lives around you with more of the fuel that ignites: joy, peace and safety.

Chapter 15: Truth, Beauty and Real Love

Let's Talk

It is so easy for us to become cynical about the power of truth, love and real beauty. We seem to be people who have adopted a mantra that life is hard. So many of us come to believe that the world is just broken and life is unfair. It would be easy to adopt such a world view. There is more than enough evidence to support such an attitude. It would be easy, but I do not believe it would be good, or wise, healthy or true. There is great beauty in the world. Think about this powerful quote from Frederick Buechner who believes the Bible calls us to surrender our cynicism:

It is a world of magic and mystery, of deep darkness and flickering starlight. It is a world where terrible things happen and wonderful things too. It is a world where goodness is pitted against evil, love against hate, order against chaos, in a great struggle where often it is hard to be sure who belongs to which side because appearances are endlessly deceptive. Yet for all its confusion and wildness, it is a world where the battle goes ultimately to the good, who live happily ever after, and where in the long run everybody, good and evil alike, becomes known by his true name....That is the fairy tale of the Gospel with, of course, one crucial difference from all other fairy tales, which is that the claim made for it is that it is true, that it not only happened once upon a time but has kept on happening ever since and is happening still.

– Frederick Buechner, *Telling the Truth: The Gospel as Tragedy, Comedy, and Fairy Tale*

Healing conversations are not something you do as an aside; they grow out of hearts that cultivate truth, beauty and real love.

Just Curious

1. In your opinion how much of an issue is cynicism in the world?

2. Where do you think it shows up most?
3. Where do you think it does the most damage?
4. How does cynicism negatively affect the culture? A family? A marriage?
5. Why is cynicism easier than optimism?

A Little Self-Disclosure

1. On a scale of 1-10 how cynical are you? Would those with whom you share relationship rate you differently?
2. Do you see others using sarcasm as humor to cover up their cynicism?
3. What do you think has inspired so much cynicism in the world?
4. Do you think the problem is a societal problem or an individual problem? Why?
5. What would have to change in order for cynicism to fade?
6. What responsibility do you believe belongs to you in celebrating truth, beauty and real love?
7. What do you imagine would happen if you committed to becoming a person who sees and celebrates truth, beauty and real love? Are there any negative outcomes?
8. How do you react to the statement that healing conversations are not an aside, but grow out of hearts that cultivate truth, beauty and real love?
9. What are your biggest take-aways from this experience?

10. What changes are you committed to making in order to grow deeper in relationship and experience more healing conversations?

Thank You, Thank You, Thank You!

Take a few minutes and allow yourself to reflect on this discussion of truth, beauty and real love. Now take a few minutes and really think back over the concepts and conversations that have been shared. What words of affirmation would you have to speak into the group? What words of affirmation would you have to speak into the process of committing to healing conversations? Take a few minutes to speak the words that you feel are most important for someone in the group to hear. Thank you for the courage to make this journey and to be vulnerable. It matters. It's how we grow!

Acknowledgments

To my family:

In all the years of writing and speaking there is a constant and ongoing need to develop content. In the heat of the moment, standing in front of a congregation and sensing that the point is not getting across, there is an immediate need for illustration. The group of people that bear a disproportionate weight for generating and having this content shared is my family. Their stories and our experiences are the first to leap to mind when the hours of study and writing need a boost. Those "funny" stories pop immediately into my head. Each family member knows the reality of a sweeping fear when a story begins in the public forum.

This book is a result of all of those years of growing and learning together. I wish to acknowledge each of them and their patience with my long learning curve and their indulgence in my attempts to thoughtfully share 'our' stories. So a special word of thanks and appreciation:

To my wife, Cyndi—Who has traveled so many years with me and has always willingly and honestly taught me about relationships.

To my four amazing daughters and now their growing families who make the challenges of life an adventure:

Amber and Bryon

Erika and Jacob, Simon and Ellie

Sunni and Austin, and Lincoln

Brandi.

Thank you to each of you! I love you!

To My Mother!

A word of appreciation to my mother who was offering me healing conversations before I could possibly understand what they were, why they mattered and how to offer them to others.

To Susan Stroh:

Without special people who bring encouragement and insight, projects like this could never be completed. You need friends to cheer for you, build up your confidence, help you get over your fears. You also need professionals who know their craft and are willing to tell you the truth about your work, or grammar, or spelling. Rarely you find someone with whom to collaborate who is both of those things and much, much more.

A very special thanks to Susan Stroh for rescuing this project when I was ready to quit. Thank you for your support and encouragement, but also for your incredible talents and gifts that have allowed me to learn the actual process of writing a book. You've worked tirelessly and brought a lot of deep thinking and refreshing laughter. You are, in every sense of the word, the best, "Writer, editor, and coach" around!

About the Author

Pastor Dave Roberts has been in ministry for over thirty-three years; the last thirty years at Montrose Church in Montrose, California. During those years Montrose Church has grown from thirty members to a ministry where more than 1500 people call this church home. In the last four years, Montrose Church has launched a second campus in Pasadena, California. Each weekend Montrose Church hosts six services over those two campuses in order to serve the needs of a growing church community.

Pastor Dave has been invited to share his message of a graceful and loving God in a variety of venues in the greater Los Angeles community, across the United States and internationally through Montrose Church's Mission partnerships.

Dave Roberts

Southern Nazarene University B.A. Religion

Nazarene Theological Seminary MDIV

CPSIA information can be obtained
at www.ICGtesting.com
Printed in the USA
BVHW072354221219
567484BV00002B/2/P

9 781642 797541